GONERS

GONERS

The Final Hours of the
Notable and Notorious

✠

BY GORDON KERR

ABRAMS IMAGE, NEW YORK

Editor: David Cashion
Designer: Alissa Faden
Production Manager: Jacquie Poirier

Library of Congress Cataloging-in-Publication Data:

Kerr, Gordon.
Goners : the final hours of the notable and notorious / by Gordon Kerr.
p. cm.
Includes bibliographical references and index.
ISBN 978-0-8109-8364-9 (alk. paper)
1. Celebrities—Death. 2. Celebrities—Biography—Anecdotes. 3. Biography—Anecdotes. 4. Death—Anecdotes. I. Title.

CT105.K393 2009
920.02—dc22
2008030407

Copyright © 2009 Gordon Kerr

Published in 2009 by Abrams Image, an imprint of Harry N. Abrams, Inc. All rights reserved. No portion of this book may be reproduced, stored in a retrieval system, or transmitted in any form or by any means, mechanical, electronic, photocopying, recording, or otherwise, without written permission from the publisher.

Printed and bound in China

10 9 8 7 6 5 4 3 2 1

Abrams Image books are available at special discounts when purchased in quantity for premiums and promotions as well as fundraising or educational use. Special editions can also be created to specification. For details, contact specialmarkets@hnabooks.com or the address below.

HNA
harry n. abrams, inc.
a subsidiary of La Martinière Groupe
115 West 18th Street
New York, NY 10011
www.hnabooks.com

FOR GAYNOR

CONTENTS

INTRODUCTION

Dylan Thomas and his famous "Eighteen straight whiskies"; Mata Hari blowing a kiss as the bullets rang out; Mary Queen of Scots dressed entirely in red. How often, when reading a biography, do you skip to the end to find out exactly how the subject died? *Goners : The Final Hours of the Notable and Notorious* dispenses with the hassle of reading the turgid details of life and takes you straight to the last days and hours of notable people—the famous and the infamous, the dictator and the demagogue, the politician and the poet.

Whether their manner of dying took the form of a vicious shooting, as in the case of the mobster Albert "Mad Hatter" Anastasia, or a quiet, dignified fade-out like ex-Beatle George Harrison; an end ridden with controversy, as in the case of Diana, Princess of Wales, or a much-mourned death that nips a promising career in the bud, such as Buddy Holly or Brandon Lee—we are as intrigued by the deaths of the notable and notorious as we are by their lives.

Goners shares the last hours of fifty famous and infamous people and explains what they were doing, who they were with, and even, in some cases, what they were wearing when they faced the final curtain. Funeral details are provided and a section for most subjects tells you what happened afterward, including the conspiracy theories that surrounded the deaths of our heroes and villains and kept them in the headlines long after their demise.

If you like trivia, *Goners* is for you; similarly, if biographies are your thing, you'll find plenty to interest you. If you're just morbidly curious—and who isn't?—there's plenty to sink your teeth into.

Above all, however, *Goners* is a book about death, and death, as we know, is endlessly fascinating.

Death means a lot of money, honey.

Death can really make you look like a star.

ANDY WARHOL

ALBERT ANASTASIA

Albert Anastasia was a creature of habit. Every day would start for him with a haircut in the barbershop at New York City's Park Sheraton Hotel. Joe Bocchino had been cutting Anastasia's short, curly hair for years and as the mobster sat down in the leather chair, Bocchino, as usual, threw a candy-striped barber's cloth around him. On a chair next to Anastasia sat a manicurist and Jimmy, the shoeshine boy, sat at his feet, working on his expensive wing-tipped shoes. It was relaxing and on this particular day, October 25, 1957, Anastasia sat quietly dozing, a hot towel covering his face, perhaps recalling incidents from his astonishing life as people quietly busied themselves around him.

He had been born Umberto Anastasio—he would later change his name to save his family any embarrassment—in 1902 in Tropea, a beautiful village on the west coast of Calabria in Italy. In his teens, he went to sea with his brother Tony, jumping ship in New York, shoeless and without a single possession to his name. By his early twenties, his notoriously short temper had already gotten him into trouble and he was sentenced to die in "Old Sparky," Sing Sing's electric chair, after killing a fellow longshoreman. But when four prosecution witnesses disappeared and others began to change their statements, a planned retrial had to be abandoned and Anastasia walked free. He had gotten away with murder.

Bootlegging during Prohibition provided him with his entrée to the world of the Mafia and he was soon working as a bodyguard for crime boss Joe "The Boss" Masseria. He later played a major part in Charles "Lucky" Luciano's rise to leadership in the National Crime Syndicate, taking part in the famous hit on his former boss Masseria in Scarpato's Italian restaurant on Coney Island in 1931. It was Anastasia who delivered the customary bullet to the head of the Mafia don as he lay dying.

His skill with a gun and his fearlessness next earned him the role of operating head of the syndicate's deadly enforcement arm, the notorious Murder, Inc. Working with psychopaths such as Louis "Lepke" Buchalter, Frank "Dasher" Abbandando, Louis Capone, Harry "Happy" Maione, Harry "Pittsburgh Phil" Strauss, Mendy Weiss, and Charles "Charlie the Bug" Workman, he personally ordered at least 63 of the estimated eight hundred murders for which Murder, Inc. was responsible. To his nickname, the "Mad Hatter," Anastasia added another: "Lord High Executioner."

By the early fifties he had ruthlessly eliminated all his rivals in the Mangano family and had claimed the top spot, a job he carried out with his customary ruthlessness and efficiency.

He began to get above himself, however, breaking the Mafia rule introduced by Bugsy Siegel that "We only kill each other" when he ordered the killing of a man who had been a witness to a robbery. "I can't stand squealers!" he exclaimed furiously, justifying the man's murder. He was also rumored to be selling membership to the family—also in contravention of mob rules—and stories of his terrible temper and violent instability were rife.

Eventually, an agreement was reached among the crime bosses and a hit was ordered on Anastasia. It was given to Joe Profaci who was believed at the time to have hired "Crazy" Joe Gallo and his brother Larry to do the job.

As he sat daydreaming in the barber's chair, three men wearing fedoras and dark glasses crept into the barbershop, pulled out .38 revolvers, and silently indicated that the barber, manicurist, and shoeshine boy should move away from the chair. They placed their legs apart, crouched slightly, pointed their weapons at the dozing Anastasia, and opened fire, shattering the early morning silence that had until then been broken only by the grumble of the occasional car from outside or the muffled noises of a hotel going about its business. As the shots rang out, the gangster instinctively raised his left hand in a futile effort to shield his head. The first bullet tore a hole right through his palm. Another couple of bullets followed in quick succession, shattering his left wrist and entering his hip.

Anastasia had risen so far in the organization that he believed himself to be immune from attack and for that reason, he no longer carried a gun. Old habits die hard, however, and he instinctively reached inside his jacket for the weapon he had carried all those years as he had clambered up the ladder of success. But his hand clutched air. Around him, the sound of exploding glass filled the room as bottles of hair pomade and lotions were shattered by the fusillade of shots.

As the three members of the hotel staff tried to make themselves part of the walls of the barber shop, Anastasia was hit again in the back as he somehow managed to raise his large body from the heavy leather chair. His eyes were by this time empty, as if the life had already left them and he turned, reaching out with trembling hands toward the shooters as if he wanted to embrace them—or, more likely, strangle them. In his confusion, he failed to realize that it was only their reflections in the mirrors in front of him that he was gesturing toward.

The striped barber's cloth still wrapped around the upper half of his body, he finally sank to the floor. One of his attackers calmly but purposefully strode over to his prone, crumpled body and delivered the customary coup de grâce, just as Anastasia had himself done all those years back to Joe Masseria—a single bullet in the back of his head.

The Funeral

Anastasia was buried in Green-Wood Cemetery in Brooklyn, New York, but he did not have the customarily extravagant gangland funeral. His family felt it was inappropriate to ask for a Mass, given the life he had led. A wake was held at Andrew Torregrossa's funeral home in Brooklyn, but there was a low turnout and watching police were disappointed not to spot any mobsters apart from Augie Pisano, who had also worked for Joe "The Boss." Anastasia was buried in a comparatively inexpensive coffin, watched by his distraught wife, Elsa, and his recently graduated son, Albert Jr. The priest who said a prayer and placed a rosary in Anastasia's hands did not even travel to the cemetery. The funeral cortege was made up of only six cars—the hearse, a car for the flowers, and four cars containing family members.

Post Mortem

As ever with gangland killings, Anastasia's murder remained unsolved. Although it was said at the time that the Gallo brothers were the shooters, recent evidence suggests that the killers may have actually been Stephen Armone, Arnold "Witty" Wittenberg, and Stephen "Stevie Coogin" Grammauta.

✠

Following Anastasia's murder, the chairs in the barbershop at the Park Sheraton Hotel were turned around to face away from the mirrors toward which he had reached out.

✠

The barber's chair in which Anastasia was attacked was auctioned off for $7,000 and was owned for many years by British-born American comedian and violinist Henny Youngman.

✠

The killings and betrayals continued.

As action heroes go, there were probably none better than Alexander III of Macedonia, a.k.a. Alexander the Great. The difference between Alexander and other so-called action heroes, such as Sylvester Stallone, Bruce Willis, and Arnold Schwarzenegger, is that Alexander did it for real. No stuntmen or body doubles for him. During his reign, he suffered at least nine wounds in battle, including a broken ankle, an arrow through the chest, and a bolt from a catapult through his shoulder. He once temporarily lost his sight after being struck on the head by a stone. He was, quite simply, a great leader who, to the disgust of other generals, unhesitatingly led his troops from the front.

On May 29, 323 BCE, however, the 32-year-old Alexander was doing what he liked best after fighting—partying. He was attending a celebration in the palace of Nebuchadrezzar II of Babylon, in honor of the death of the greatest of all mythical Greek heroes, Heracles.

Alexander had returned six months earlier from his victorious Indian campaign, but recent bad omens and prophesies had clouded preparations for his latest initiatives—the irrigation of the Euphrates and a campaign in the Persian Gulf to settle the Arabic coast, due to begin on June 4.

There were twenty A-list guests at the dinner, among them Ptolemy, King of Egypt; Perdiccas, one of Alexander's generals; Eumenes, the royal secretary; Philip, the royal doctor; Alexander's engineer, Nearchus, who had just been appointed admiral for the Persian Gulf expedition; and Peucestas, his son.

During the dinner Alexander displayed his learning—and perhaps his memory—by reciting an extract from *Andromeda*, a play by Euripides. Then he drank wine from the "cup of Heracles" which was traditionally circulated at these events, toasting the health of all twenty men present. He filled a huge beaker with a large measure of unmixed wine (normally, it was diluted with water) and threw it back heartily.

Shortly afterward, perhaps slightly the worse for wear given the amount of wine he had consumed, Alexander decided it was time for bed. However, he was persuaded by his close friend, Medius, to come and have a few more drinks with him. Not long after, the king left the party, drowsily taking a bath and finally going to sleep. But you can't keep a good man down, and, before long, he was back drinking with Medius long into the night. Once again, Alexander bathed and went to bed. By this time, however, he was suffering from a slight fever.

The next day, the fever was such that he was not well enough to walk and he had to be carried out to perform his daily religious duties. Afterward he lay in his quarters until sundown, issuing orders to his officers. He was then carried down to the river Euphrates and taken across by boat to the park on the other side, where he rested.

In the morning Alexander offered sacrifices, still issuing orders to his troops making ready for the departure to Persia. In the evening he ate a little and went to bed, his fever mounting.

The following few days continued in this vein, Alexander slipping deeper and deeper into fever as the hours passed. By June 8, his condition was grave, but in spite of his increasing weakness, he persisted with his religious duties and preparations for the imminent departure of his army.

The following day, he was moved back across the river to the palace. By this time he was very ill and no longer able to speak, although he could still recognize his commanders when they entered his room. For the next 24 hours his fever remained high and his soldiers became anxious. Rumors spread that he was already dead and that his guards were keeping it secret. They insisted on seeing their leader, forcing their way into his tent. As he lay speechless, his troops filed silently past him. It is said that at this point, Alexander's commanders asked him who should succeed him. He is reported to have replied: "The strongest man."

Shortly after, close to sunset on June 10, 323 BCE, the solemn announcement was made outside the royal tent that Alexander the Great, having conquered vast swathes of the known world during his twelve years and eight months' reign, was dead, at age 33.

Post Mortem

Perdicas became regent until the birth of Alexander's son, Alexander IV.

✠

Alexander was honored as a god, both in Egypt and in the cities of Greece.

✠

Ptolemy I transported Alexander's body to the Egyptian city of Alexandria.

✠

Several centuries after his death, his golden sarcophagus was melted down to make coins by Ptolemy IX and replaced with one made of alabaster.

✠

Many notable people paid their respects at Alexander's tomb, including Julius Caesar, in 45 BCE. Augustus visited the tomb in 30 BCE, following his victory over Mark Anthony and Cleopatra and his conquest of Alexandria. According to a report by a Roman historian, when Augustus bent over to kiss Alexander, he fell forward and accidentally broke the corpse's nose. Caligula also visited and left with Alexander's cuirass. The tomb was closed to the public in the third century CE, six centuries after Alexander's death, because of the huge numbers of visitors and fears that it would be damaged.

✠

Alexander's alabaster sarcophagus vanished during the fourth century CE.

✠

In 1995 a tomb was discovered in the oasis of Siwah. It was initially thought to be Alexander's, but this view is now generally held to be incorrect.

THE CONSPIRACY THEORY

When Alexander died, it was not thought that he had been

murdered. Six years after his death, however, it was suggested that there had indeed been a plot to kill him that night. In on the plot, it was claimed, were his friend Medius; Iollas, his butler; Nearchus, his admiral; Philip the doctor; and others.

The plot was planned, it was suggested, by the Macedonian general Antipater, after advice from the philosopher Aristotle, who had been one of Alexander's teachers. Cassander, Antipater's son, traveled to Babylon in the last months of Alexander's life and is thought to have brought poison with him from Greece, which he gave to his brother Iollas. Iollas, in his position as Alexander's butler, was perfectly placed to mix the poison into the royal wine. It was certain that Alexander would be the first to drink from the cup of Heracles and, on that night, everything went exactly as planned. It was reported that after the king drank, "all of a sudden, he shouted with pain as if struck through the liver with an arrow." He could only bear the pain for a few minutes before leaving the room where the party was taking place.

At 7 A.M. on September 11, 1973, Salvador Allende, the Marxist president of Chile, awoke to the news that two units of the Chilean navy had rebelled at Valparaiso, and had taken control of two of the country's three cruisers. Influential elements in the country had finally grown tired of his socialist policies—the nationalization of American-owned copper multinationals and extensive land reform. Soaring inflation and widespread shortages, caused in part by a U.S. trade embargo, had created an increasingly unstable situation and a growing economic crisis. Now, it seemed the army and the people had simply had enough, and within half an hour, Allende was speeding toward La Moneda, the presidential palace, a cohort of armed police flanking his car during the hour-long journey.

At La Moneda, he immediately delivered a broadcast on the country's left-wing radio stations, urging the Chilean people to remain in their factories and at their desks. He went on to say that he fully expected the armed forces to remain "faithful to their tradition" and to support the government by crushing the naval rebellion—a pretty forlorn hope, as it turned out, but he repeatedly insisted that he would not resign.

At 8:20 A.M., one of his air force generals called to inform him that a plane was waiting to take him out of the country. But as uncompromising as ever, Allende refused the offer and ordered him to do his duty.

At 10:30 A.M., the military junta broadcast an ultimatum, demanding that he resign.

By 11 A.M., Allende had made the decision that the only way he would leave the palace would be dead and he announced this to stunned colleagues. Speaking to the Chilean people once more on the radio, he said he would "resist by all means, at the cost of my life; to leave to the ignominy of history the lesson of those who have force but not reason." This phrase reflected the Chilean national motto—'*Por la razon o la fuerza*'—(by reason or force).

Things became even bleaker for Allende when it became apparent that not a single unit of the Chilean armed forces had remained loyal to him. Consequently, La Moneda's civilian staff began to evacuate the building, leaving Allende, wearing a helmet and armed with a machine gun, personally directing the two hundred or so policemen who stayed with him.

At noon, an aerial bombardment began and armored cars surrounding La Moneda opened fire. At least twenty bombs fell on the palace and soon it was ablaze. Additionally, armed helicopters opened fire on the roofs and upper stories of the high buildings on either side of it. Just after two o'clock, an infantry patrol burst into the second floor of the palace. Arriving at the door, Captain Roberto Garrido, commanding the soldiers, saw through the smoke a group of civilians who were armed with submachine guns. He ordered his men to open fire on them and one member of the group was hit in the stomach, falling to the floor in agony.

Realizing that the person who had been hit was in fact

Allende, an excited Garrido shouted: "We shit on the President!" Another burst of machine-gun fire riddled Allende with bullets and he fell back, dead. At that point another group of civilians burst in, pursuing the soldiers down to the first floor.

Dr. Enrique Paris, Allende's personal physician, examined the president, finding at least six bullet holes in his abdomen and lower stomach. When he signaled that the president was, indeed, dead, a Chilean flag was produced and used to cover the body.

Allende's last words to the Chilean people had been: "Probably Radio Magallanes will be silenced and the calm metal of my voice will not reach you. It does not matter. I have faith in Chile and in her destiny. Others will surmount this gray, bitter moment in which treason seeks to impose itself. You must go on, knowing that sooner rather than later, the grand avenues will open along which free people will pass to build a better society."

THE FUNERAL

Allende was buried anonymously, but 15 years after his death, in a "gesture of reconciliation," his successor, General Augusto Pinochet, allowed a funeral to take place. His body was exhumed and placed in a new casket and, amid great emotional outpouring, a memorial service was held in Santiago's cathedral.

POST MORTEM

Between 6 and 8 A.M. on the day of Allende's death, about six thousand leaders of towns, unions, farmworker settlements, political parties, and leftist cultural organizations throughout Chile were arrested. Prisoners were taken to military headquarters, interrogated, and executed immediately afterward. The military described this as "cleaning up the motors of Marxism."

✠

Resistance in Vicuña Mackenna and Los Cerrillos was fierce, weakening only when the worker's ammunitions gave out. Mass murders in Santiago's working class districts finally put an end to the resistance.

✠

It had been the intention of the military to tell the world that Allende had committed suicide. After the fierce resistance at La Moneda and elsewhere, however, they stalled for more than twenty hours. Finally, the news was leaked abroad and Chileans learned from foreign correspondents that their president had "committed suicide."

✠

The great Chilean poet Pablo Neruda died and was buried two weeks after Allende's murder. His funeral gave the Chilean people the opportunity to express their vehement opposition to the Pinochet regime.

✠

A four-man military junta, headed by General Pinochet, took over in Chile. Pinochet immediately instigated a program of mass arrests and political assassinations. Most of the businesses and farms nationalized by Allende were restored to private ownership. In 1989 Pinochet lost in a plebiscite on whether he should be allowed to stand in the upcoming election and was succeeded as president by Patricio Aylwin.

JOHN BELUSHI

By the early 1980s John Belushi's drug intake was spiraling out of control, raising concerns among friends and associates who recognized a strong self-destructive side to this larger-than-life character. Many concurred with what *Saturday Night Live* writer Michael O'Donoghue said of him around this time: "The same violent urge that makes John great will ultimately destroy him."

On March 4, 1982, Belushi was excited because he had finally been given the opportunity to expand his horizons and stabilize his career at the same time. It had certainly been an astonishing career so far. Born in 1949 to immigrant Albanian restaurant owners, he had been a performer from an early age, achieving cult stardom through his brilliant performance in the 1978 film *National Lampoon's Animal House* and his appearances on NBC's top-rated satirical television show, *Saturday Night Live*. A *Saturday Night Live* sketch, "The Blues Brothers," performed with fellow comedian Dan Ackroyd, was made into a hugely successful film. In the debit column, however, were commercial failures such as the 1981 film *Continental Divide* in which Belushi plays a reporter investigating a corrupt Chicago councilman.

The source of Belushi's excitement was the offer of a serious role in the film *Once Upon a Time in America*, to be directed by the great Italian director Sergio Leone. Not only did it offer a chance to prove that he could handle dramatic roles as well as comedic ones, but best of all, he would be sharing the screen with the great Robert De Niro. He must have been serious about it because he had even agreed to shed forty pounds for the part.

That Thursday night, however, Belushi was engaged in his favorite pursuit—having fun. He dined with De Niro on Sunset Strip, no doubt discussing the film that would bring their two talents together, before going on to a show at West Hollywood's Improv club in the company of his girlfriend Cathy Smith, a former backup singer with rock group the Band, and *Saturday Night Live* writer Nelson Lyon. Leaving Improv, the trio staggered to another club, On the Rox, where Belushi jammed onstage with Johnny Rivers. They then went next door to the Rainbow Room to eat. When Belushi began to complain that he felt ill, they decided to return to their hotel. People who saw him that night claim he was on a relentless cocaine high. For John Belushi this was nothing out of the ordinary.

He was in no state to drive so one of the others drove his Mercedes back to Bungalow 3 at the Chateau Marmont Hotel in West Hollywood, where, for the past week, he had been staying with Smith. He was helped indoors and once there, immediately went to the bathroom and threw up. That represented nothing more than a mere inconvenience, however, as he resumed drinking wine and inhaling and injecting cocaine. According to Smith, Belushi asked her to inject him with a needle full of drugs several times that night and, although normally terrified of needles, he seemed to be enjoying the high he got from them.

At some point in the proceedings, comedian Robin Williams,

who was no stranger to cocaine in the 1980s, dropped by, but he was wary of Smith and wondered why Belushi was hanging out with someone like her. As he left, Williams joked with Belushi, "If you ever get up again, call."

Then, sometime after 3 A.M., De Niro knocked on the door but, taking a look at what was going on in the room, he quickly made his excuses and left. Meanwhile, the booze and drug binge continued.

Around 6:30 A.M., Belushi took a shower and finally at around eight in the morning he went to bed. Cathy Smith recalls that he lay on his right side, shaking and wheezing from a sinus problem. At 9:30, she heard loud sneezing coming from the bedroom and went in to check if he was alright. He told her he was fine. She gave him a glass of water and he went back to sleep.

Looking in again at 10:15 A.M., she saw that he was covered by a blanket and he seemed to be sleeping. By this time, however, she was hungry and took the Mercedes to get something to eat.

At 12:30 P.M., Belushi's physical trainer, Bill Wallace, who had been helping him to lose weight, arrived at the bungalow to find the actor comatose in his bed, lying in a tight fetal position. Wallace was immediately concerned because he knew Belushi was an inveterate snorer, but on this occasion he was not making a sound. Realizing Belushi was in trouble, Wallace immediately cleaned out the star's nose which was filled with mucous, lay him on the floor and called for help.

The paramedics arrived too late, however, and at 12:45 P.M. it was announced that John Belushi had become a fully paid-up member of a clique that he had once joked about on *Saturday Night*

Live—the "live fast, die young, leave a good-looking corpse" clique. In this case, the corpse probably did not look so good.

The Funeral

John Belushi was buried on March 10 in Abel's Hill Cemetery on Martha's Vineyard. His fellow Blues Brother, Dan Akroyd, led the procession on his motorcycle and as it began to snow, James Taylor sang "That Lonesome Road."

A memorial service was held the next day at the Cathedral of St. John Divine, during which Akroyd played a tape of the Ventures's guitar instrumental, "The 2000 Pound Bee," the fulfillment of a pact the two had made earlier in the year to play the song at each other's funerals.

In May of 1983, Belushi's widow had John's coffin moved to an unknown location in the cemetery because fans were desecrating his grave. During the operation, John's wooden casket collapsed and a copper one had to be used instead.

Post Mortem

The coroner judged Belushi's death to have been caused by "acute cocaine and heroin intoxication" but Cathy Smith admitted in an interview in the *National Enquirer* that she had administered a speedball—a mixture of cocaine and heroin—to the star. The authorities pounced and she was indicted for first-degree murder for her role in the injection of the lethal doses that killed Belushi. She fled to Canada and fought extradition until 1986 when she was convicted of manslaughter, spending 18 months in prison.

BILLY THE KID

Born in 1859 in the slums of New York City, like countless others, Henry McCarty traveled west with his mother following the death of his father. They arrived in Silver City, New Mexico, in 1873, but by 1877 McCarty was in Lincoln County, New Mexico, going by the name of William Bonney.

Lincoln County was a byword for anarchy at the time. The Apaches had been tamed and cattlemen were now fighting each other for local power. Unfortunately, Bonney allied himself to the losing side, working as a ranch hand for a rancher named John Tunstall, who became something of a father figure for the young man. When Tunstall was ambushed and killed in 1878 by a sheriff's posse, the legend of Billy the Kid began as Bonney set out on a campaign of revenge for Tunstall's murder.

Patrick Floyd Garrett had been a buffalo hunter in Texas before drifting into New Mexico and being elected sheriff of Lincoln County in 1880 to restore justice to the area. One of the first things he did was arrest Bonney, who had spent the past two years hunting down and killing a number of Tunstall's murderers, including Garrett's predecessor as sheriff and his deputy. By the time the young outlaw was convicted and sentenced to hang, it was reckoned that he had killed at least 21 men.

But, while Garrett was away on county business, Bonney attacked one of his guards and escaped, shooting two men in the process and leaving town on a stolen horse.

Claiming that he had been promised a pardon by Governor Lew Wallace in exchange for information about other killings, Bonney escaped as far as a friend's ranch at Fort Sumner, about a hundred and forty miles west of Lincoln County. Garrett set off in pursuit of the Kid, accompanied by two of his deputies, John Poe and Thomas McKinney.

On the night of July 14, the three men approached the former fort that had been converted to living quarters. Because the residents sympathized with the Kid and refused to provide Garrett with information, the sheriff decided to find Peter Maxwell, an old friend and the son of Lucien B. Maxwell, a New Mexico land baron. He thought Maxwell might give him the information he needed.

They rode toward Maxwell's property, stopping nearby. They unsaddled their horses, had some coffee, and then went into an orchard that ran down to a row of old buildings, some sixty yards from Maxwell's house. Approaching these houses, they could hear people inside speaking in Spanish. After a short while, a man stood up. He was wearing a broad-brimmed hat, dark waistcoat, and trousers, and was shirt-sleeved. He spoke a few words, went to the fence and jumped it, and walked toward a house.

Unknown to Garrett and his deputies, this man was Billy the Kid. He entered the house—it belonged to a Mexican friend — removed his hat and boots, and stretched out on a bed, reading a newspaper. Soon, however, he woke up his friend who was asleep in the same room and told him to get up and make some coffee. He added that he was hungry and asked for a butcher's knife so that he could go over to the Maxwell house to get some beef. The Mexican gave him a knife and the Kid, hatless and barefoot, set off on the short journey to Peter Maxwell's house.

Garrett still did not recognize the Kid as he left the orchard. He and his men retreated a short distance and, trying to avoid the houses, approached Maxwell's house from the opposite direction. Arriving at the porch, Garrett told Poe and McKinney to stay where they were, and he went into the house.

It was close to midnight and Maxwell was already in bed. Garrett approached the bed in which he was lying, sat down on it, and asked him in a hushed voice if he knew where Billy the Kid was. Maxwell told him that the Kid had been there but he had no idea if he still was. Just then, a man sprang quickly into the doorway, shouting in Spanish, "Who's there?" When there was no reply the man stepped cautiously into the dark room, holding a gun in his right hand and a knife in the other.

As he approached the bed, Garrett leaned down and whispered: "Who is it, Pete?" But Maxwell did not answer. For a moment, Garrett thought it might be Maxwell's brother-in-law, Manuel Abreu. Perhaps he had seen Poe and McKinney outside and wanted to know what was going on. The intruder came close and leaned down, both hands on the bed, his right hand almost touching Garrett's knee in the darkness. He asked in a low voice: "Who are they, Pete?" At that moment, Maxwell whispered to Garrett: "That's him!" The Kid, realizing there was another man present, raised his pistol about 12 inches away from the sheriff's chest. He then retraced his steps back across the room, shouting in Spanish: "Who's that?" Garrett wasted no time. He drew his revolver rapidly and fired into the darkness in the direction of the words. Throwing his body aside, he fired again. There was no point in the second shot. Just 21 years old, Billy the Kid was already dying as he fell to the ground.

THE FUNERAL

Billy the Kid was buried at Fort Sumner and shares a plot with his friends Charles Bowdre and Tom O'Folliard. The grave actually has two tombstones. The first was erected in 1932, purchased by Charlie Foor, a pallbearer at the Kid's funeral. The second tombstone was erected in 1940. The main tombstone is inscribed "Pals."

POST MORTEM

Pat Garrett was shot and killed near Las Cruces in 1908 in a dispute over grazing land. His body lies in the Masonic cemetery in Las Cruces.

✠

Garrett's image is part of the logo on Lincoln County Sheriff Department's uniforms.

✠

Garrett's daughter, Elizabeth, wrote "O Fair New Mexico," the state song.

THE CONSPIRACY THEORY

Ollie "Bushy Bill" Roberts of Hico, Texas, but living in New Mexico in 1950, claimed for years to be William Bonney and demanded the pardon he had been promised by Governor Wallace.

It is claimed that it was Pat Garrett himself who smuggled the gun into jail that Billy the Kid used to escape. This theory claims that the body that was buried was actually a drunk named Billy Barlow who was shot in the face by Garrett and the Kid to prevent recognition. A man named Homer Overton swore an affidavit that he had been told this story in 1940 by Garrett's widow, Apolonaria, when he was just nine years old.

Overton's sworn statement was offered in support of a failed move to exhume the body of Catherine Antrim, the Kid's mother, so that her DNA could be compared with Bushy Bill's.

KAREN CARPENTER

In 1983 Karen Carpenter was living in a condominium in Los Angeles, fittingly at 2222 Avenue of the Stars, while her brother, Richard, the other half of the phenomenally successful singing duo the Carpenters, lived in Downey, near the house they had built for their parents.

The siblings had enjoyed major pop success, touring the world and selling some eighty million records. Their personal lives were far from happy, however. Richard was addicted to sleeping pills and for many years, Karen had battled anorexia nervosa. In Richard's words, she had actually been a "chubby teenager," but by the autumn of 1975, after years of gorging herself on thyroid and laxative pills and throwing up what little food she ate, she weighed only around eighty pounds. When she walked onstage, audiences gasped at how thin she was. She had to lie down between shows and that same year had collapsed onstage in Las Vegas while singing "Top of the World." She was a long way from the top of the world when she was finally admitted to a hospital in the mid-1970s. But doctors and therapists could do little to help her.

It was at her parents' house that Karen spent the evening of February 3. She ate her last meal with them at Bob's Big Boy restaurant, in Downey. Somewhat predictably, she had a Caesar salad.

The next morning, she got up, put on a red jogging suit in

the pocket of which was a vial of Ativan—a drug that belongs to the class called benzodiazepines, which are generally used for sedation and anxiety disorders. She went into the kitchen at approximately 8:45 P.M. and five minutes later her mother found her unconscious on the floor.

Paramedics were called and took her to the Downey Community Hospital where, in spite of the doctors' best efforts, she was pronounced dead at 9:51 P.M. of a cardiac arrest, brought on by the strain the anorexia had put on her heart. She was 32 years old and weighed 105 pounds.

THE FUNERAL

On the morning of February 5, Karen's body was taken to the Utter McKinley funeral home where a viewing was held on the following Sunday. Her casket was cream-colored and remained closed, with a photograph placed on top by Richard. The funeral service took place at the Downey United Methodist Church, and although only six hundred were invited, a thousand mourners turned up. Among those present were Olivia Newton-John, Burt Bacharach, and Dorothy Hamill. The service was broadcast to the crowds outside and included an instrumental version of a Carpenters medley, including "Rainy Days and Mondays" and "We've Only Just Begun." Karen was buried in Forest Lawn Memorial Park in Cypress, California, and on her crypt is the legend: "A Star on Earth—A Star in Heaven."

POST MORTEM

On December 11, 2003, Richard had the bodies of Karen and

their parents exhumed and reinterred in Pierce Brothers Valley Oaks Memorial Park in Westlake Village, California, because he had bought a new house there, putting a whole new meaning into the words of their hit song, "Close To You."

NICOLAE AND ELENA CEAUŞESCU

I n Woody Allen's hilarious *Bananas*, Allen, who has somehow become a South American dictator, announces that all
men are from now on to wear their underpants outside their
trousers. It would have come as no surprise if Nicolae Ceauşescu, who had become president of Romania in 1967, had made
a similar pronouncement.

In 1966, for instance, he banned abortion, birth control, and
divorce, decreeing that all Romanian women must bear five
children apiece. As a result, state-run orphanages were soon
filled to overflowing with about one hundred and fifty thousand
orphans in a country with a population of only five million.

Ceauşescu's paranoia unleashed many other bizarre policies and practices on an increasingly impatient and confused
Romanian people. He would only wear clothes that had been
stored under guard in a warehouse; he promoted a Labrador
retriever to the rank of colonel in the Romanian army, giving it
its own house, telephone, and motorcade; he had all typewrit-
ers registered so that he could trace any abusive letters and,
after shaking the hand of Queen Elizabeth II on a 1978 visit to
England, washed his own with alcohol to get rid of germs.

On December 16, 1989, the dissident Laszlo Tokes, an ethnic
Hungarian Lutheran minister, became the focus of a massive
anti-Ceauşescu protest in the Transylvanian city of Timişoara.
The city's inhabitants had been angered by Tokes's forced reloca-

tion, but the mob's chants of support for Tokes soon turned into "We want bread" and "Down with Ceauşescu."

When he was told of the protest, Ceauşescu flew into a violent rage and began ranting about a plot against him, planned by his old enemies the Soviets and the Americans. He sent in the army and violence erupted with more than a hundred protesters being massacred. Ceauşescu had miscalculated, however. The Timoşoara revolt very quickly erupted into a nation-wide uprising against the government.

To counter it and to try to regain control of the situation, he organized a pro-government rally in Bucharest. His plan dramatically backfired when the crowds at his rally failed to do as he wanted and they too began to protest against him on live television.

Fighting broke out in Bucharest between antigovernment forces and the Securitatae, the national security force that was reported to have kept almost 15 percent of the population as paid informants.

Senior army generals and many Communist party figures joined the protests and the tide quickly began to turn in favor of the protesters. The Securitatae were swiftly defeated, in spite of a system of underground tunnels that had been built specifically for them under the streets of the city.

On Friday, December 22, Ceauşescu and his wife Elena attempted to flee in a helicopter to Iran, but it was forced to land. They were finally captured in a car about sixty miles from Bucharest.

Brought before a tribunal, the couple was charged with genocide, armed attack on the people, abuse of state power, the destruction of buildings and state institutions, and undermining and obstructing the national economy. They refused to collaborate, claiming the tribunal had no authority over them. Instead, they demanded to be tried by Romania's Grand National Assembly as the members of the tribunal were only ordinary citizens. "You can shoot us if you like, but we do not recognize you as a court," the 71-year-old dictator said. The trial proceeded, nonetheless, the dictator appearing calm throughout and even smiling occasionally, although his face was gaunt and unshaven. By contrast, Elena's expression was vacant. She stared blankly straight in front of her and failed to react even when her husband patted her leg in an effort to comfort her.

At the end of the two-hour tribunal, the prosecutor summed up the feelings of the Romanian people: "Esteemed Mr. Chairman, I have been one of those who, as a lawyer, would have liked to oppose the death sentence, but it would be incomprehensible for the Romanian people to have to go on suffering this great misery and not to have it ended by sentencing the two Ceauşescus to death. The crimes against the people grew year by year. They were only busy enslaving the people and building up an apparatus of power. They were not really interested in the people."

The elderly couple were sentenced to death by firing squad.

When news of the verdict leaked out, more than three hundred soldiers volunteered to take part in the firing squad, keen to avenge the sixty thousand lives that had been lost during the Ceauşescu regime. However, only three were chosen—an officer and two privates—by lottery.

The Ceaușescu's last wish was to die together and at 4 P.M. on Christmas Day, 1989, that wish was granted. As the couple were led out to their execution, Elena said to one of the soldiers, "I was like a mother to you." "What sort of a mother were you, who killed our mothers?" was his bitter reply.

"The anti-Christ died. Oh, what wonderful news!" was the way one Bucharest radio announcer announced the executions.

Post Mortem

The location of the tribunal and the executions was never made known, for fear of action by remnants of the Securitatae.

✠

The summary nature of the executions fueled rumors that the Ceaușescu were silenced to protect others.

✠

There was some criticism of Romania's new leaders from abroad. The strongest came from the United States. "We regret the trial did not take place in an open and public fashion," said a U.S. statement. Britain, however, was more straightforward and even sympathetic. "It was a civil war situation and the normally accepted standards of legality hardly obtained at the time. Although one may regret a secret trial, at the time it was not really surprising," said a foreign office spokesman.

✠

An impromptu governing coalition, the National Salvation Front (FSN), proclaimed the restoration of democracy and freedom. They dissolved the Communist party, transferred its assets to the government, and repealed bans on private commercial entities and independent political activity.

✠

Elections were held on May 20, 1990, and Ion Iliescu, FSN leader, former Central Committee secretary, and deputy member of the Political Executive Committee, who had fallen out of favor with Ceauşescu , won the presidency with 85 percent of the vote.

ANTON CHEKHOV

Anton Pavlovich Chekhov, perhaps the most popular Russian writer outside his own country, had suffered from tuberculosis since his early teens. By 1897 it was so bad that he had gone to live in the Crimea where the climate was more suitable.

In 1904, at age 44, Chekhov traveled to Europe, accompanied by his wife Olga Knipper, a star of the Moscow Arts Theatre, to fight the increasing ravages of his illness. They stayed at the Sommer Hotel in the health resort of Badenweiler in southern Germany's Black Forest and enjoyed the services of a local German doctor named Schwoerer.

Coincidentally, two young Russian brothers, acquaintances of the Chekhovs, were also staying at the hotel. Leo Rabeneck was a student whose brother had fallen ill in Berlin when the two were en route from Moscow to Switzerland. A doctor had recommended a period of convalescence in Badenweiler, and the brothers had taken rooms at the Sommer Hotel. Recognizing Olga Knipper at breakfast one day, they recalled that they had been guests at the same time as the Chekhovs at Lyubimovka, the estate of Stanislavsky, the great Russian theater director.

Olga invited the brothers to drop in on her husband who, she said, was "very homesick for Russia and for the company of his fellow countrymen." In spite of her claims that her husband's health was improving, however, when Leo Rabeneck visited the writer he was struck by "the discrepancy between this seeming improvement—for he had very good color and was very sunburnt—and the impression he gave at the same time of general exhaustion." He recalled that Chekhov coughed frequently and spat into a small spittoon, which he carried in the pocket of his jacket.

Chekhov remained optimistic about his condition, even making plans for his return to Russia, but his restlessness soon began to show. On June 29, he wrote to his sister Masha: "I just can't get used to German silence and calm. I've got a tremendous longing to go to Italy."

Not long after, a heat wave struck southern Europe—the worst weather for a man in the grip of advanced tuberculosis—and on July 12, Chekhov suffered the first of two heart attacks. Nonetheless, he still seemed to rally. Then on the evening of Thursday, July 14, events began to move rapidly. Rabeneck was resting after a walk in the hills around Badenweiler when Olga called him. She asked him to go and fetch Dr. Schwoerer, who arrived to find Chekhov breathing with such difficulty that he had to be given oxygen. As he was doing this, Schwoerer whispered to Rabeneck to go downstairs and fetch a bottle of champagne from the hall porter. In those days, it was medical etiquette for a doctor to offer champagne when all hope was gone.

When the champagne arrived, Chekhov sat up in bed and said: "*Ich sterbe!*"—"I am dying!" The doctor poured out an almost full glass and gave it to the writer who smiled and said, "I haven't drunk champagne in a long time." He downed the liquid in one gulp and the doctor handed the empty glass to Rabeneck. As Rabeneck turned to place the glass on the table, he heard a sound come from Chekhov's throat, a sound he later described as "rather like the noise a watertap makes when air gets into it."

It was only when the doctor let the writer's hand fall that Rabeneck realized that Anton Pavlovich Chekhov was finally dead.

THE FUNERAL

Chekhov's remains were locked up in a refrigerated train car marked "Oyster Wagon" and shipped back to Russia from Germany for burial.

The writer Maxim Gorky was at the funeral at the Novodeviche Monastery in Moscow with Chekhov's sister Masha and his widow. He wrote, "I am so depressed by this funeral. As if I was smeared by sticky, foul-smelling filth. People climbed trees and laughed, broke crosses and swore as they fought for a place. They asked loudly, "Which is the wife? And the sister? Look, they're crying." The singer Chaliapin, burst into tears and cursed: "And he lived for these bastards, he worked, taught, argued for them."

POST MORTEM

When he died, Chekhov's body had not been laid out correctly and in the morning Rabeneck and Schwoerer were unable to straighten it, the writer's head remaining slightly turned to one side.

✠

In order not to upset the hotel's other guests, the body was not removed to a local chapel until the next night. Instead of a stretcher, a laundry basket was used which was too short for the writer's body to lie flat. Therefore, he had to be put in it in a half-sitting position. Rabeneck wrote: "I walked behind the men carrying the body. Light and shade from the burning torches flickered and leaped over the dead man's face, and at times it seemed to me as if Chekhov was scarcely perceptibly smiling at the fact that, by decreeing that his body should be carried in a laundry basket. Fate had linked him with humor even in death."

PATSY CLINE

Patsy Cline had flown to Kansas City to perform her special brand of country music at a concert to raise money for the family of disc jockey "Cactus" Jack Call. Call had recently been killed in a car accident and perhaps the fact that the 34-year-old singer had herself almost died in a car crash several years previously had persuaded her to perform.

But on the Monday after the concert, March 4, 1966, Patsy was not feeling well and skipped breakfast. She had been awake all night coughing and a friend persuaded her to ride back to Nashville with her and her husband in their station wagon instead of flying back in the single-engine Piper Comanche PA-24 owned by her manager, Randy Hughes, in which she had flown to Kansas from Nashville. She even brought her bags down to the hotel lobby but then abruptly changed her mind. She said she felt a sense of loyalty to Hughes and would, after all, fly back with him.

That day the storms that were raging in across the plains were of such severity that they were prevented from taking off. Their departure was postponed until the next day when, at around 1:30 P.M., Patsy, Randy Hughes, and fellow performers Hawkshaw Hawkins and Cowboy Copas boarded the flight.

By 5 P.M., when the plane made a refueling stop at Dyersburg Municipal Airport, a small airport in northwest Tennessee, they had already had to land and take off several times, once running into a severe hailstorm. The Federal Aviation Authority was describing the weather as "extremely turbulent" and thunderstorms had passed over the airport in the mid afternoon, with more following just before the Piper Comanche had landed. The airport's operators, Bill and Evelyn Braese, both veteran pilots, urged the singer's party not to continue their journey. Bill Braese even offered them the airport courtesy car and suggested that he would fly their plane to Nashville the next day when the weather had improved.

But Patsy wanted to get back to Nashville, and while she, Copas, and Hawkins headed for the airport restaurant inside the terminal building, Hughes put in an order for fuel. In the restaurant, Patsy drank an iced tea and ate shrimp salad. Onlookers spotted her wearing a red trouser suit and it has been said that her great hit "Crazy" was playing on the jukebox. It was the last song she heard.

Meanwhile, Hughes phoned his wife to be told that the weather in Nashville was fine. Unfortunately, it was fine only because Nashville was in the eye of a storm.

They took off again at 6:07 P.M., but even without the storm this was something of a gamble, because at that time in March it was already beginning to get dark. Fatally, Randy Hughes was not trained to fly in the dark.

Seventy miles west of Nashville, above Camden, Tennessee, Hughes lost visibility, and the plane started to nosedive. Investigators surmised that he was trying to land on a nearby highway, but the aircraft hit some trees on the way down and crashed in a hollow in a wooded area called Fatty Bottom, just west of Camden, probably at a speed of between two hundred twenty and two hundred sixty miles per hour. Patsy Cline and her three traveling companions were killed instantly.

The Funeral

Patsy's husband, Charlie Dick, brought her body home for viewing in a closed casket in her living room, and a prayer service, attended by twenty-five thousand people, was held for all four victims on Thursday, March 7. Patsy was buried on Sunday, March 10, in Shenandoah Memorial Park in her hometown of Winchester, Virginia.

Post Mortem

The plane was found by William Jeffrey Holdsworth and his son, Jeners. Wreckage was strewn over a two hudred fifty-yard area and as word spread of its location, hundreds of onlookers converged on the area, looking for souvenirs and carrying off personal effects. By Sunday, three thousand people had visited the scene and one report says someone even took a shoe with a human foot still in it.

✠

Randy Hughes and country superstar Jim Reeves had taken lessons from the same flight instructor. A year after the Patsy Cline crash, Reeves was killed in identical circumstances.Friends claimed later that Patsy had premonitions of her death, saying that she did not expect to live to the age of thirty. Shortly before her death she had established a trust fund for her children.

✠

An inscribed boulder marks the sight of the crash.

✠

When two pieces of the plane were recently put up for auction
on eBay, the bidding reached $51,100 before complaints
persuaded the Web site to pull the auction.

BOB CRANE

On June 28, 1978, Bob Crane was playing the Windmill Dinner Theatre in Scottsdale, Arizona, the latest leg of his tour with the play, *Beginner's Luck*. It had been seven years since the credits had rolled for the last time on *Hogan's Heroes*, the phenomenally successful World War II prison camp comedy in which he had played the starring role, and they had been difficult years. His *Bob Crane Show* had been terminated after only three months and a couple of films he had starred in for Disney, *Superdad* and *Gus*, had flopped miserably.

Crane had bought the rights to *Beginner's Luck* in 1973. He produced it and starred in it, and was taking it on tour around the entire country. As ever, in Scottsdale he was carousing with his old friend John Carpenter, a video equipment salesclerk he had known for years. They had been introduced while Crane was in *Hogan's Heroes,* and shared a mutual interest in topless bars and strip clubs, Crane's particular penchant being for buxom women.

As if his love life was not complicated enough, an affair with Cynthia Lynn, the actress who had played Colonel Klink's secretary in *Hogan's Heroes*, was followed by a fling with another actress, Patti Olsen, which led to him walking out on his marriage of 21 years and marrying Patti. Now, in 1978, he was in the process of divorcing her.

Carpenter loved it when Crane came to town. The actor's

fame was like a magnet for women and once they had hit the bars and nightclubs and picked up a couple of women, they were in the habit of taking them back to Crane's apartment and filming themselves having sex. All was not well, however, by June 1978 and Crane decided to call time on his friendship with the video salesman, especially as he believed that Carpenter had recently made a pass at him.

On this particular Wednesday night, after finishing his evening performance and signing autographs, Crane returned with Carpenter to his apartment. There he received a phone call from his estranged wife. They argued loudly.

The two men then went to a local bar where they had arranged to meet a couple of women. At about two in the morning, the four repaired to the Safari coffee shop, Carpenter leaving about thirty minutes later to pack for his return trip to Los Angeles the following morning. Carpenter called Crane from his hotel room and it is thought that it was during this phone call that Crane, tiring of the heavy partying and hangers-on, told Carpenter that he would not be seeing him again.

Next morning, Crane's costar in *Beginner's Luck*, Victoria Berry, arrived at his apartment. There was no reply to her knocking and, the door being unlocked, she let herself in. Entering the bedroom, she found Crane dead in bed, clad only in boxer shorts and so badly beaten that he was unrecognizable. "At first, I thought it was a girl with long dark hair," she said, "because all the blood had turned real dark. I thought, 'Oh, Bob's got a girl here. Now where's Bob?" I thought, "Well, she's done something to herself. Bob has gone to get help." Then she realized that it was blood. "The whole wall was covered from one end to the other with blood. And I just sort of stood there and I was numb. He was curled up in a fetus position, on his side, and he had a cord tied around his neck in a bow."

He had been bludgeoned to death and around his neck, the killer had tied an electric cord. Bob Crane was 49 years old.

THE FUNERAL

Crane was buried in Oakwood Cemetery, in Chatsworth, California. *Hogan's Heroes* costars Larry Hovis, Robert Clary, and Leon Askin attended.

His body was exhumed and moved to Westwood Memorial Park by his second wife, Patti, without telling Crane's children. There is a rumor that he was divorcing her so that he could go back to his first wife, the children's mother. His body lay in an unmarked grave until 2003.

POST MORTEM

Neighbors are reported to have heard nothing and there were no signs of a struggle, leading police to believe that Crane was asleep when attacked.

✠

Video equipment and a library of videos were found in the apartment showing Crane and Carpenter engaged in group sex with different women.

✠

Police described it as "a well-planned murder," their investigation immediately focusing on Carpenter, who was one of the last people to see Crane alive. He also phoned the apartment from Los Angeles while the police were there and was told that they were investigating an incident. Strangely, Carpenter did not ask what kind of incident. Blood matching Crane's, a rare blood type, was found in the car that Carpenter had rented. However, in the days before DNA matching, it was hard to prove that it was Crane's and the county attorney did not wish to proceed with a prosecution against Carpenter. The police were later accused of mismanaging the investigation.

Under "Cause of Death" on Crane's death certificate is written simply "Head Injury."

Fourteen years after the murder, in 1992, it was determined that fat tissue found in the rental car were a match with that found in the apartment. The police also decided that Crane was killed with a camera tripod that was visible in the videotapes, but had been missing from the apartment when his body was found. Charges were brought against Carpenter, but he was acquitted.

John Carpenter died in 1998, still denying any involvement in Bob Crane's death.

Crane died a wealthy man, having secured a percentage of revenues from *Hogan's Heroes*.

THE CONSPIRACY THEORY

Bob Crane was a light sleeper, and there were no signs of forced entry. The county medical examiner therefore surmised that Crane knew his killer, and that it was someone who had been there earlier and had reentered the apartment through a door or window that he had left unlocked. There was cash in Crane's wallet, suggesting that robbery was not the motive. Due to the coldness of the body and the onset of rigor mortis, the medical examiner stated that Crane had been killed in the early morning.

There was a bottle of scotch on the table; Crane never touched scotch.

There were rumors that Carpenter had borrowed fifteen thousand dollars from the actor and Crane was now demanding repayment of the loan.

The killer had to be very strong as the lack of blood on the ceiling suggested a short swing of the murder weapon. A weaker person would have required a larger arc and blood would have sprayed out from the wound.

One theory suggests that a jealous boyfriend or husband of one of Crane's conquests murdered him.

A tire on Crane's car was tampered with during his last performance that night. It is thought that it was intended to strand him in the dark theater parking lot.

JOAN CRAWFORD

By 1970, Joan Crawford had done just about everything a Hollywood screen goddess could be expected to do. A stellar career, complete with Academy Awards, followed by burn out— she was described as "box-office poison"—followed by a dramatic comeback; four marriages, one of them to Douglas Fairbanks Jr.; an affair with James Stewart; the bitch-war with Bette Davis; the marriage to the chairman of the Pepsi-Cola Company and the board position after his demise; the rumors about her bisexuality; the miscarriages; the adoptions.

Now, however, the movie parts had dried up, especially after her last, disastrous film, *Trog*, described by one critic as "worse than bad." She turned up at a party for Rosalind Russell in 1974 and then the erstwhile Lucille Fay LeSueur disappeared from public view, taking to retirement and seclusion in an apartment on the 22nd floor of Imperial House on New York's Upper East Side.

By 1977 Joan knew the end was not far away. After the death of her beloved poodle, Clicquot, she replaced him with a shih tzu, Princess Lotus Blossom. But two days before her death, too ill to look after her, she gave the dog away to friends. Bedridden for months, she was suffering from cancer of the pancreas and also had serious heart problems. She weighed just 85 pounds.

In the last years of her life, she had become a Christian Scientist and every day, she was visited by a Christian Science practitioner who prayed with her and read to her from the writings of Mary Baker Eddy. Having dismissed her maid, Mamacita, the previous week, she was being cared for by a couple of loyal fans.

That last day, Tuesday May 10—coincidentally the 22nd anniversary of her marriage to Alfred Steele, Chairman of Pepsi-Cola—one of these fans, arrived at apartment 22-H at around 8 A.M. She realized very quickly that the star was fading fast and began to pray. Joan overheard her. "Dammit!" she exclaimed, "Don't you dare ask God to help me!"

With that, she had a heart attack and died.

THE FUNERAL

Joan Crawford's funeral took place on Friday, May 13, 1977, at the Frank Campbell Funeral Home. She was embalmed and then cremated, the urn being placed on a pedestal in the chapel while a Christian Scientist read the service. Myrna Loy, Van Johnson, and Andy Warhol were present.

Her urn was put with her husband's at Ferncliff Cemetery and on Tuesday, May 17, Pepsi-Cola held a memorial service for her in New York to which, besides Joan's children, Anita Loos, Geraldine Brooks, Cliff Robertson, and Pearl Bailey turned up. A minute's silence was called for her on all Hollywood lots the Friday after her death.

Another memorial service was held on June 24 in the Samuel Goldwyn Theater at the Academy of Motion Picture Arts and Sciences, attended by John Wayne, Robert Young, Myrna Loy, and Stephen Spielberg. Jack Jones sang "Everything I Have is Yours" from Joan's 1933 film, *Dancing Lady*. Delivering the eulogy, the great Hollywood director George Cukor said: "She was the perfect image of the movie star. I thought Joan Crawford would never die. Come to think of it, as long as celluloid holds together and the word Hollywood means anything to anyone, she never will."

POST MORTEM

Joan cut her adopted children Christina and Christopher out of her will. It is said that she knew about the book Christina was writing, *Mommie Dearest*, a scathing account of an abused childhood, published in 1978 and eventually made into a film starring Faye Dunaway. The children sued and got a settlement of $55,000. Interestingly, Joan's other adopted children said that the picture of Joan given in *Mommie Dearest* was inaccurate.

✠

In November 1998, when *Mommie Dearest* was republished, Christina hired a drag queen who looked like Joan to accompany her to book signings.

✠

At an auction of Joan's personal effects in 1978, Andy Warhol bought her false eyelashes.

THE CONSPIRACY THEORY

Several of Joan Crawford's friends, as well as Fred Lawrence Guiles's biography, *Joan Crawford: The Last Word,* claimed that she committed suicide. They pointed to the way she gave away a great many of her possessions as well as her dog in the months and days before her death. The coroner said that he had no reason to doubt that she died of heart failure, but her friends base their suspicions on the facts that there was no autopsy and that she was cremated. There was, therefore, no evidence.

In 1975 Joan had received an anonymous phone call: "I will kill you. You won't know where or when, but I will get you." She called in the police and the FBI and her apartment was under surveillance for months. She had sophisticated locks and alarms installed and her bedroom door was bolted every night. She was so terrified she did not set foot outside her apartment in the last 18 months of her life.

BING CROSBY

B ing Crosby's astonishing career wound down as the austere 1950s turned into the swinging sixties. Then as the sixties drew to a close, this most prolific of recording artists stopped recording altogether; by then it had been many years since he had toured. In 1973, however, a health scare seemed to galvanize him back into action. He was taken to a hospital, suffering from chest pains and fever, and a tumor was removed from his left lung.

To the great joy of his millions of fans, he began to record and perform live again. But his health suffered another setback when in March 1977, during a televized concert celebrating his fiftieth year in show business, he fell backward into the orchestra pit, rupturing a disc and enduring a month-long stay in the hospital. He was soon back on the road again, appearing in Europe and taping a Christmas special, in England, somewhat incongruously starring David Bowie. Following that, he recorded what was to be his last album, *Seasons*. A two-week engagement at the London Palladium followed and then a concert in Brighton on October 10, his last-ever appearance. On the next day, Bing guested on the Alan Dell radio show on the BBC, singing eight songs. Later that day, he had a photo shoot for the cover of *Seasons*.

The day after, October 12, Bing flew to Spain where he planned to play golf and hunt. Thus, on October 14, he was playing the La Morajela golf course near Madrid where he and a partner were taking on a couple of Spanish golf pros. A doctor in England had told Bing that he should only play nine holes of golf due to his ill health but this day, Bing knew better and played the whole 18.

He played well, too, shooting a very credible 85, as he and his partner won the match after handicaps had been taken into consideration. After sinking his last putt, around 6:30 P.M., he bowed to the other players' applause and said: "That was a great game of golf, fellers." Then they stepped off the 18th green, where, "Suddenly he dropped," said his partner, professional golfer Juan Tomas Gandarias. "Before that he had given no sign of illness although he seemed to be favoring his left arm near the end of the game."

They were about twenty yards from the clubhouse and as he fell he banged his head on the red brick path, raising an ugly bruise. His golfing companions carried him to the clubhouse where a physician administered oxygen and adrenalin without success. He had died of a massive heart attack at age 74.

THE FUNERAL

U.S. consular officials arranged for Bing's body to be taken to the U.S. Air Force base at Torrejon, outside Madrid. An American mortician was flown in to prepare the body for its return to the United States.

His will insisted on a private funeral. So to avoid the expected media scrum, it began at 5 A.M. on October 18 at St. Paul's Roman Catholic Church in suburban Westwood, California.

He had stipulated that only his wife and seven children should attend, but Kathryn Crosby invited Bing's siblings as well as Bob Hope, Rosemary Clooney, and Phil Harris. Crosby's body lay in an open oak casket which was adorned by a single spray of red roses, and his six sons acted as pallbearers.

He was buried at the Holy Cross Cemetery in Culver City, California, where his headstone reads: "Beloved By All. Harry Lillis 'Bing' Crosby. 1904 -1977," even though it is now clear that he was actually born in 1903. He is buried next to his first wife, Dixie Lee, and his parents, and close to the graves of Mack Sennett, Pat O'Brien, Ray Bolger, Jack Haley, Spike Jones, and Jimmy Durante.

POST MORTEM

A few hours after learning of her husband's death, Kathryn Crosby issued the statement: "I can't think of any better way for a golfer who sings for a living to finish the round."

✛

Bing Crosby was one of the wealthiest entertainers in Hollywood. He had property in Florida, as well as music holdings, and was also a part owner of the Pittsburgh Pirates baseball team. He had interests in numerous businesses, including real estate; frozen orange juice, mines; oil wells; cattle; racehorses; a racetrack; music publishing; professional baseball, football, and hockey teams; prize fighters; radio and television stations; banks; and television and film production companies. At his death he was probably worth in excess of $150 million.

✛

Bing left money for all of his children, but there was a catch. It was left in a blind trust until they turned 65. Dixie Lee, his first wife, had left her money to her four sons, but it ran out in 1984.

✠

Six years after his father's death, Bing's son Gary wrote a book, *Going My Own Way*, which shocked the world. Gary wrote about years of physical and emotional abuse from his father, from his nickname of "Bucket Butt," to weekly weigh-ins and beatings that drew blood. Gary said in the book that to help him endure the pain, he would dream up ways to kill his father. Gary's brother Lindsay supported the charges in the book. However, Bing's second family was outraged.

✠

Gary Crosby died of lung cancer at age 62. Dennis and Lindsay both shot themselves. Phillip is a nightclub owner and vehemently denies that Bing was a bad man. Nathaniel, the third of Bing's kids with his second wife, Kathryn Grant, shared his father's love of golf. For several years, while still in his teens, he ran the Bing Crosby golf tournament founded by his dad. In 1981 he was U.S. amateur champion and he traveled on the European golf tour for three years.

ED DELAHANTY

They say that Ed Delahanty could strike a baseball hard enough to split it in two. A leading slugger of the late nineteenth and early twentieth centuries, he is one of the few players to have hit four home runs in one game, and he also boasts one of the best records of consecutive hitting, with a streak of more than thirty games. His great prowess on the diamond, however, was marred by a disastrous personal life blighted by alcohol and gambling and a mental instability that would, unfortunately, prove fatal. On numerous occasions, he threatened to kill himself, and his mother became so concerned about him that she would often follow him when his team went on the road, to make sure he came to no harm.

In 1900, baseball's senior league, the National League, was in turmoil. Players' wages were being reduced and teams from Washington, Baltimore, Louisville, and Cleveland were dropped from the league. Byron Bancroft "Ban" Johnson saw his opportunity and started up a rival operation, the American League, offering players better salaries and launching teams in major cities such as Boston and Baltimore. Many of the National League's star players defected to the American League and Ed Delahanty, popularly known as "Del," was seen as a very attractive prospect, with most of the fledgling league's teams making him offers. To begin with, he remained with his team, the Philadelphia Phillies, mainly because of a record-breaking new contract.

The next year, however, he agreed to sign for the American League's Washington Senators, receiving a four thousand dollar advance. It was good news for the bookies, because much of that four thousand ended up in their pockets. His first year was good, and at age 35 and in his 16th season as a professional, he was the League's batting champion. Around this time, New York Giants manager, John McGraw, arrived on the scene to entice Del with a huge offer—$24,000 for three seasons. He grabbed it.

But he would never play for the Giants. An agreement between the National and American Leagues in January 1903 included the return of Delahanty to the Senators and he returned reluctantly to Washington. It was not a good season. His average fell and he failed to turn up for games. He was drinking heavily and on one occasion he had to be dragged from his hotel room by a teammate after turning on the gas. He was briefly suspended and then reinstated. Then, on June 25, the Senators traveled to Cleveland.

His drinking on this trip turned monumental and his teammates grew very concerned. His behavior became increasingly erratic—one night he drove a teammate from his hotel room at knifepoint. The Senators headed for Detroit where his condition deteriorated still further.

On June 29, he failed to show up for the game, and on the following day, he sent his wife, Norine, a telegram asking her to meet him in Washington when the Senators returned home. In a letter he also sent her he described an insurance policy he had taken out on himself. In the letter he expressed a macabre wish that the train would derail on the journey home—he hoped it would be "dashed to pieces" and he along with it.

But he failed to make it back to Washington. The day before the party was due to leave Detroit, he disappeared from the team hotel and they returned without him. However, this was not the first time Del had gone missing—six years earlier he had vanished for a week and turned up in Cincinnati.

Initially it was thought his disappearance was a ploy to engineer a return to the Giants. Other ballplayers had successfully employed this tactic. However, by July *The Washington Post* was running the headline: WHERE IS DELAHANTY? and his family and friends were becoming concerned. Their concern was increased by a letter that arrived on July 6. It was from a district superintendent at a railroad company informing them that Del had been thrown off a train at Fort Erie, Ontario, after behaving violently towards the conductor. The letter went on to say that the bridge night watchman had found a man behaving strangely on the International Bridge that carries the railway line across the Niagara River—between Fort Erie and Buffalo. The man had reacted angrily when the watchman had shone a lantern in his face and he had run off. Shortly after, the night watchman heard a splash. The letter informed them that the man's suitcases had been left behind on the train and had been found to contain a Washington Senators complimentary pass, in the name of Ed Delahanty.

It later emerged that Del had been drinking whiskey heavily on the train and had begun to act wildly. He had pulled a woman from her berth by the ankles and was wielding a razor in a threatening manner. When the conductor and a number of other men ejected him from the train, the conductor warned him, "Don't make any trouble, you know you're still in Canada." Del had replied, "I don't care whether I'm in Canada or dead."

Seven days after the incident on the bridge, Ed Delahanty's body was found by a dockworker at the *Maid of the Mist* landing stage on the Ontario side of the gorge. His body had made the long journey down the Niagara River and over the Horseshoe Falls. The body had been badly mutilated during its time in the water. The stomach was split open, Ed's intestines hanging out, and a propeller blade—probably belonging to the *Maid of the Mist* —had almost severed his left leg below the knee. He was wearing only a silk necktie, shoes, and socks.

THE FUNERAL

The funeral was held on July 11 at the Church of the Immaculate Conception in Cleveland, and he was buried at Cavalry Cemetery. His four ball-playing brothers, Jim, Frank, Joe, and Tom, attended, as well as numerous friends from around the leagues. John McGraw, manager of the New York Giants, served as a pallbearer.

POST MORTEM

The insurance policy had run out by the time of his death and Delahanty left his family destitute. Officials of the Senators and the American League organized benefits and donated money personally to his family.

✛

Norine sued the railroad company at the end of the season and was awarded an unsatisfactory $5,000.

✚

Ed Delahanty was inducted into baseball's
Hall of Fame in 1945.

THE CONSPIRACY THEORY

Delahanty's family suspected foul play and the night watchman, Sam Kingston, came under suspicion. However, Kingston was seventy years old and it is hard to imagine him getting the better of a fit, albeit drunk, professional baseball player. Nonetheless, at the time of his death, Del had been carrying a diamond ring, a diamond tiepin, a gold watch, and some other valuable trinkets, as well as around $200 in cash. These had all disappeared. Strangely, Kingston had arrived home that night wearing Delahanty's hat.

Kingston said that Del had threatened him with a piece of coal, but there was no coal on or anywhere near the bridge.

Kingston said that he had heard Del cry for help, but he unaccountably took no action. He merely continued on his rounds, failing to report the incident until the next morning.

Not long after Delahanty's body was discovered, the same dockman at Niagara Falls found the body of a local farmer in the same place. The $1,500 he had been carrying had disappeared.

DIANA
PRINCESS OF WALES

On the morning of Saturday, August 30, Diana, Princess of Wales, sat enjoying the sunshine and chatting with her friend Rosa Monckton on the deck of the *Jonkal*, the yacht of her boyfriend, Dodi Al Fayed, moored off Sardinia's Emerald Coast. When breakfast arrived—coffee, croissants, and jam; a basket of bananas, apples, grapes, oranges, and kiwis—Diana drank her usual large glass of fresh orange juice and poured hot milk in her coffee. She was relaxed, tanned, and very happy after the Mediterranean idyll they had just enjoyed.

As they ate, Dodi received a call on his mobile phone from Frank Klein, president of the Ritz Hotel, which was owned by Dodi's father, Mohammed Al Fayed. Klein also managed the Windsor Villa, the former residence of the Duke and Duchess of Windsor, which Dodi's father had been leasing from Paris city officials since 1986. Dodi informed Klein that he wanted to move into the villa, explaining that his "friend"—if you had been reading the tabloids, you did not have to be a genius to work out who this "friend" was—no longer wanted to live in England. "We want to move into the villa, Frank," said Dodi, "because we are getting married in October or November." The two men agreed to meet in Paris the following Monday to discuss the matter.

Having accompanied Diana back to Paris, at around 6:30 Dodi went to the boutique of the jeweler Alberto Repossi to collect the $200,000 engagement ring that he had bought for Diana and which Repossi was resizing. Although the shop was less than a hundred yards from the hotel, Dodi's obsession with security led him to insist on being driven there in his Mercedes 600. He was accompanied by Diana's bodyguard, Trevor Rees-Jones, who waited in the car while Dodi went into the shop.

Inside, Dodi spotted another ring he thought she might like and asked Repossi if he could take both away with him to find out which the princess preferred. They returned to the hotel's Imperial Suite where Dodi decided after all on the original ring—from a range called "Tell Me Yes."

Diana and Dodi had planned to eat dinner that evening at Chez Benoit, a fashionable restaurant near the Pompidou Center. Stopping first at Dodi's ten-room apartment on the Rue Arsene-Houssaye, close to the Arc de Triomphe, they changed their minds when they spied the crowds of paparazzi waiting for them and decided instead to return to the Ritz to eat. Even there, however, the throng of tourists and photogra phers was so great that they could only open the car door with difficulty. A security man recalls: "The cameras were right next to her face. Once inside, she sat on a chair and looked as if she were about to cry." Diana was distressed and Dodi was furious.

It was now almost 10 P.M. and Henri Paul, acting head of Ritz security, was summoned. Paul had already met the couple at the airport earlier in the day, transporting Dodi's luggage to the Arc de Triomphe apartment. He had gone off duty at 7:05 P.M., but now rushed back to the hotel. Critically, it is not known what Paul did in the hours when he was away from the hotel. Even more critically, it is not known how much alcohol he consumed.

Back at the hotel, he was in the Vendôme bar and said by Wingfield to have been drinking "pineapple juice, which he cut with water from a carafe, because he found it too strong." Diana's bodyguard, Rees-Jones, later told police that Paul had been drinking a yellow liquid. That liquid turned out to be pastis.

At 11:15 Dodi announced that he had a plan to fool the paparazzi. His regular car and driver, plus a backup vehicle, would leave from the front of the hotel and act as decoys, while Diana, Dodi, and Rees-Jones would drive off secretly from a rear exit with Paul at the wheel of a Mercedes S-280. In July he had employed the same scheme, but the main difference was that on that occasion his own chauffeur had been at the wheel.

After dinner, he called his father and explained his plan. Mohammed Al Fayed said he was not happy with it, suggesting instead that they remain at the Ritz for the night. But Dodi refused. He had made up his mind and seemed excited. Diana and he were later seen on the Ritz's CCTV cameras laughing and joking as they waited to make their exit.

It went wrong immediately. By the time the Mercedes stopped at traffic lights in Place de la Concorde, half a dozen photographers had caught up with it. Paul put his foot down just before the light changed and the Mercedes sped off onto the river-front expressway toward the Alma tunnel.

About thirty seconds later he inexplicably lost control of the car and it crashed headlong, at high speed, into the tunnel's 13th pillar. The Mercedes spun around and came to rest against the north wall, its horn blaring from the weight of Paul's dead body, which had slumped over the steering wheel. He and Dodi were killed instantly and Diana and Rees-Jones were seriously injured. The impact had been so great that parts of the car's radiator were found in Paul's body.

Within seconds the paparazzi arrived and began taking pictures. The photos show Diana with blood on her forehead, but with her face unmarked. Dodi's body is on her lap and her left arm is draped over his kidskin boot.

It took 15 minutes for the first fully equipped ambulance and its onboard doctor to arrive. Removing the princess was then a slow, delicate operation. Emergency workers had to cut through metal because one of her legs was pinned under the seat. Her condition was stabilized at the scene of the crash and an ambulance then carefully drove her the 3.8 miles to the hospital.

On arrival, she was still breathing, but when doctors opened her chest they found massive hemorrhaging from a torn left pulmonary vein. Doctors fought desperately to save her, repairing the wound and massaging her heart manually for two hours, but at 4 A.M. Diana, Princess of Wales, was pronounced dead at the age of 36.

THE FUNERAL

Diana's funeral took place on Saturday, September 6, at Westminster Abbey amid scenes of extraordinary hysteria and sadness. Huge crowds gathered outside the Abbey and in Hyde Park, where the service was relayed on a huge screen. Elton John sang a specially rewritten version of his song, "Candle In the Wind," and Diana's brother, Earl Spencer, delivered a bold and moving eulogy that berated the paparazzi and the royal family in equal measure. "Of all the ironies about Diana," he said, "perhaps the greatest is this: that a girl given the name of the ancient goddess of hunting was, in the end, the most hunted person in the modern age." Taking a swipe at the royals who had taken away Diana's title of "Royal Highness," he said that his sister possessed "natural nobility [and] proved in the last year that she needed no royal title to continue to generate her particular blend of magic." He vowed that his family would ensure that Diana's sons, William and Harry, were brought up "so that their souls are not simply immersed by duty and tradition but can sing openly as [Diana] planned." The crowds outside the cathedral broke into spontaneous applause. The service ended with a minute's silence that echoed around the land.

Later, as Diana's hearse made its way to her family's estate 75 miles away in Althorp Park for a private burial, the huge crowds lining the roadsides showered it with flowers. The private service on an island in the middle of a lake was attended by no more than ten mourners, including Princes Charles, William, and Harry.

POST MORTEM

As flowers piled high outside Kensington Palace, the royal family were vilified for their treatment of Diana. Eventually, the Queen calmed the situation by giving a televized speech on the Friday after the crash, speaking of her grief and her loss. The Queen offered to return posthumously Diana's former title, "Her Royal Highness." Earl Spencer rejected the offer.

The paparazzi were initially cleared of blame by the courts. All blame was directed at the driver, Henri Paul. It was stated that he was drunk and taking antidepressants at the time of the accident. The judges determined that he had to avoid a slower-moving car as he entered the tunnel –the elusive white Fiat Uno which, in spite of police investigating more than four thousand owners of Fiat Unos, has never been found.

In the four weeks after the funeral, a report by the Oxford Centre for Suicide Research found that the overall suicide rate in England and Wales rose by 17 percent.

✠

The "Tell Me Yes" ring was later found in Dodi's apartment, still in its unopened box. It now lies in a safety deposit box in a Swiss bank, along with several love letters from Diana to Dodi. In early 2005, Surrey coroner Michael Burgess opened and adjourned for a year inquests into the deaths of Diana, Princess of Wales, and Dodi Al Fayed, pending the results of a police inquiry into the crash that killed them.

The 2008 inquest into the deaths of Diana and Dodi was sensational and hugely expensive. The jury ruled that the couple were killed unlawfully due to the actions of driver Henri Paul and the paparazzi. The inquest found that Paul was well over the French blood alcohol limit; Diana was not pregnant; the white Fiat Uno did indeed exist, and Diane and Dodi's car struck it a glancing blow; the three who died in the car were not wearing seatbelts; there was no plot by Prince Philip and/or MI6 to kill Diana despite evidence by Dodi's father in which he described Prince Philip as a "nazi" and a "racist," the royal family as that "Dracula family" and Camilla Parker-Bowles, Prince Charles's wife, as a "crocodile wife"; Diana did fear for her life—Lord Mishcon, Diana's lawyer, told of a conversation with her in which she claimed that the Queen was going to abdicate in favor of her son Charles and that she was to be sidelined by a car accident.

THE CONSPIRACY THEORIES

In his book, *A Royal Duty*, Diana's former butler Paul Burrell published a handwritten letter in which Diana claimed someone was planning to kill her in a car accident by tampering with her brakes.

There were 28 errors in Henri Paul's postmortem, and no investigation into a suspiciously high carbon monoxide reading in his blood.

It is claimed that the crime scene was not properly preserved; that the Mercedes was removed from the tunnel with "indecent haste"; and that initially the French police were either ignorant or lied about a collision with a second car, the mysterious Fiat Uno.

There are serious unanswered questions, some claim. These include why it took medical rescuers nearly two hours to get the princess to a hospital; why French authorities have not made available tapes from surveillance cameras outside the Ministry of Justice (next door to the Ritz) and along the Mercedes' route; and why the British intelligence service has failed to come forth with what they know about the crash. Investigators were said to have examined enlarged still photos taken from the Ritz security videotapes to identify suspicious men outside the hotel, apparently neither photographers nor tourists, shortly before Dodi and Diana fled from the rear.

Conspiracy theorists speculate that a motorcycle worked with the Fiat Uno, pursuing the Mercedes doggedly from the Place de la Concorde, forcing it to drive faster as it approached the tunnel. There definitely was a motorcycle right behind the Mercedes, and it does not appear to have been driven by a photographer. Three witnesses, all of whom were in the eastbound lanes, described seeing a large motorcycle in the westbound lanes slow down and pass the wreck just moments after the crash.

Suspects in Diana's death are listed variously as:

1. The royal family, who with the aid of the British Secret Service and Parliament, and perhaps the CIA and FBI, conspired to deny a Semitic foothold to the throne. This was exacerbated by the claim that Diana was already pregnant with Dodi's child. Also, the government had been growing tired of Diana's security expenses.

2. The Pope, who recognized that the impending union of British and Arab interests threatened the security of the Vatican hegemony. This would have meant a fundamental shift in the balance of power.

3. International arms merchants who had begun to feel the financial bite of Diana's campaigns against the use of land mines.

4. Diana, herself, who obsessed over her late beau, distressed by the possibility of a second divorce, and wanting to possess Dodi forever, arranged the romantic tragedy.

5. Di and Dodi, who faked their deaths and in a twist of perfect irony, sold photos of their "accident" to the tabloids for millions. They now live in quiet retirement on an island, finally free of the paparazzi who plagued them.

CHARLES DICKENS

In the summer of 1870, Charles Dickens was spending time at his home, Gad's Hill, near Rochester, working on his last and ultimately unfinished work, *The Mystery of Edwin Drood*. On Monday, June 6, he walked his dogs into Rochester to buy a copy of the *Daily Mail*. His daughter Katie was visiting Gad's Hill and was taking his other daughter, Mamie, back to London with her that day for a short visit. As they were leaving, Katie went to take her leave of her father, now back at his desk, writing. Dickens hated farewells and normally when he was working, he would merely raise a cheek to be kissed. On this occasion, however, he stood up, took her in his arms and said: "God bless you, Katie." She never saw him alive again.

That afternoon, he rode into the village of Cobham with his sister, choosing to walk home through the park, and after dinner, he spent the evening in the sitting room, looking at some Chinese lanterns, bought that day, which were now lit in the conservatory. He chatted with his sister about how much he loved Gad's Hill, how he wanted his name to be forever associated with the place, and how he wanted to be buried nearby.

On the morning of June 8, Dickens awoke in good spirits. He intended to work on *Edwin Drood* all day and his morning was spent in the chalet where he worked. He returned to the house for lunch and, afterward, smoked a cigar in the conservatory before returning once more to the chalet.

Before dinner, he seemed to his sister to be tired, silent, and distracted. However, he was often like this when he had been working hard. While waiting for dinner, he wrote some letters in the library and dealt with some business matters related to meetings he was to have in London the following morning. He planned to travel there later that night.

When they sat down to dinner, his sister was shocked at his paleness. She asked him if he was ill and he replied that he had not felt well for about an hour. He would not let her send for the doctor and insisted on carrying on with dinner. He also insisted that he would still travel to London later.

Dickens was, in fact, having a stroke and though he fought hard against it, continuing the conversation, his speech became incoherent and indistinct. He was obviously ill and his sister begged him to go to his room while she summoned help. "Come and lie down," she pleaded. "Yes, on the ground," he replied before falling to the floor. It was a few minutes after six and those were the last words he uttered.

A couch was brought in on which he was laid, and a messenger was sent to fetch the local doctor. Telegrams were sent to his family and his daughters were summoned. They arrived later that night and kept watch by his bedside. His feet were cold and hot bricks were placed by them, but Dickens never moved and never opened his eyes again.

On the afternoon of June 9, the celebrated London physician Dr. Russell Reynolds arrived but could only confirm the verdict of the two doctors already in attendance, that there was no hope for the great writer. That evening, at ten past six, Dickens's daughter said that as she watched, she saw "a shudder pass over our father, he heaved a deep sigh, a large tear rolled down his face and at that instant his spirit left us."

The Funeral

Dickens had wanted to be buried in the churchyard at Shorne, but the dean and chapter of Rochester Cathedral requested that he be buried there. When that had been arranged, another request came that the writer's last resting place should be in Westminster Cathedral. His daughters asked only that a clause in Dickens's will should be adhered to: "I emphatically direct that I be buried in an inexpensive, unostentatious, and strictly private manner."

And so it was that on June 14, 1870, Charles Dickens, writer of *Oliver Twist, David Copperfield,* and *Great Expectations* was buried in Westminster Cathedral with just a few friends and family present.

Hundreds of people visited the grave in the weeks after his death and flowers continued to be sent, both from Britain and overseas, for many years.

JOHN DILLINGER

Manhattan Melodrama is a gangster film made on a modest budget about the relationship between two childhood friends, one of whom grows up to be a gangster, the other a district attorney. The movie was moderately successful on its release in 1934 but was notable for several reasons. It starred Clark Gable, about to receive his only Oscar for Best Actor for his previous film, *It Happened One Night*, and it featured the first of 14 screen pairings for the bankable duo William Powell and Myrna Loy. It was also the last film watched by the notorious bank robber John Herbert Dillinger. As he left the Biograph Theater in Chicago, he was ruthlessly gunned down by waiting FBI agents.

During the early 1930s, Dillinger captured the imagination of the American public. At a time when banks were low in the public estimation—the Depression having forced many out of business, taking with them people's life savings, and when others were foreclosing on businesses and homes as the economy continued to falter—anyone getting one over on them was guaranteed to achieve a level of popularity. John Dillinger and his gang of ruthless killers did just that. Accompanied by men such as the psychopath "Baby Face" Nelson, Dillinger became idolized as he carried out swashbuckling bank raids and daring prison breaks across America.

He and the two gangs with which he was associated over

the years stole around $300,000, about $5 million in today's terms—a large sum now, but an unbelievably huge amount of money at the time of the Depression.

For his troubles, Dillinger went to prison a number of times but always managed to break out, in 1934 getting out of Crown Point prison in Indiana—supposedly escape-proof and guarded by large numbers of police officers and national guardsmen—using a gun fashioned out of soap or wood, depending on who you listen to, and blackened with shoe polish.

It was this incident that would lead to Dillinger's demise. Driving over the Indiana-Illinois state line in a stolen car, he finally placed himself firmly in the jurisdiction of Herbert Hoover's fledgling FBI, created specifically to deal with the menace of "public enemies" such as Dillinger.

The bank robberies resumed and the gang narrowly escaped while they were hiding in Wisconsin. Even surrounded by FBI agents, however, and with a reward of $20,000 on Dillinger's head, they managed to escape yet again.

Then in the summer of 1934, Dillinger vanished. When police found his car on a side street in Chicago, they surmised he was at large in the city. He was actually in Chicago going under the assumed name of Jimmy Lawrence. Working as a clerk, he was living a fairly anonymous existence and dating a girl named Polly Hamilton.

Sunday, July 22, 1934, was boiling hot, almost a hundred degrees. Word had come to the feds that Dillinger would be going to a movie that afternoon, in the company of two women, Polly Hamilton and Anna Sage. Sage was a Romanian brothel-keeper, original surname Cumpanas, who was under threat of deportation back to her native country. Unknown to Dillinger, she had made a deal with the authorities—she would give them Dillinger if they would lift the deportation order. She informed them of his movements that Sunday.

Manhattan Melodrama was showing at the Biograph Theater in Chicago's Lincoln Park area and the three were spotted entering the theater, Dillinger paying. Outside waited around twenty G-Men, led by the head of the Chicago FBI office, Melvin Purgis. The plan was for Purgis to light a cigar when he saw Dillinger and the women leave the Biograph. That would be the signal for the start of the operation. The program would last two hours and four minutes, with newsreel footage and advertisements added to the movie.

Purgis was nervous and aroused suspicions from the woman in the ticket booth as he repeatedly checked the exit. She informed the theater manager who, fearing a robbery, called the police. When they arrived a few minutes later, Purgis sent them packing, flashing his badge and informing them that a stakeout was taking place.

At the appointed time, Dillinger emerged from the theater, strolling casually between the two women. Purvis gave his signal and as he lit the cigar, Dillinger glanced at him, but didn't suspect anything. Agents swiftly moved in, surrounding the gangster as Purgis called out in a nervous voice: "Stick 'em up, Johnnie! We have you surrounded!"

Dillinger instinctively reached for the gun that was secreted in the pocket of his pants—it had been too hot to wear a jacket

—but it was too late. He fell to the ground in a hail of bullets in an alley beside the theater. Two bullets had grazed his face, close to his left eye. A third bullet hit his left clavicle and exited through the left side of his body. The fourth bullet—the one that killed him—entered the base of his neck, traveling upwards and exiting close to his right eye. He died without saying a word, at age 31 years and one month.

THE FUNERAL

John Dillinger's body was taken to Alexian Brothers Hospital where it lay on the lawn until he was declared dead by the deputy coroner. The corpse was then transported to Cook County Morgue. On Tuesday, July 24, Dillinger's father and half-brother traveled with a hearse containing the body across the Indiana border to the Harvey Funeral Home in Mooresville. The authorities provided a police escort—perhaps they thought Dillinger had one more audacious escape up his sleeve.

The casket was taken to the home of Dillinger's sister, Audrey Dillinger Hancock, in Maywood, Indiana, where it was put on show in her living room for about an hour, and people were allowed into the house to see it. Meanwhile, large crowds of curious people thronged the neighborhood. Police became so concerned by the size of the crowds that they persuaded the Dillinger family to hold the funeral as quickly as possible.

On Wednesday, July 25, John Dillinger was laid to rest during a raging thunderstorm in Crown Hill Cemetery in Indianapolis. The grave had a police guard to prevent the theft of the body until a few days later, when the grave was reopened and concrete, mixed with chicken wire and scrap iron, was poured on top of the coffin. There was no chance of escape for Dillinger this time.

POST MORTEM

The souvenir hunters had already struck by the time Dillinger's body arrived at the morgue. His clothes were already gone and a large ring he had been wearing had disappeared from his finger. In the alley, people dipped their handkerchiefs in Dillinger's blood, creating gruesome keepsakes. Others had more mercenary aims. There was only $7.70 in his pockets when he died, but it was claimed that he habitually carried thousands of dollars on him. It has been suggested that a police officer called Zarkovich, who had been close to Anna Sage, removed the cash from the body.

✠

Crowds swarmed to the Cook County Morgue where the autopsy was carried out. The postmortem room was thronging with doctors, nurses, police officers and FBI agents, newspapermen, society people, politicians, and many others. Hundreds more gathered outside. Dillinger lay on the slab, wrapped in a winding sheet as they filed past him, women screaming and shrieking as they looked at his wounded face. Fifteen thousand people are said to have viewed the body.

✠

When the body arrived at Audrey's house, she was initially not convinced that it was her brother—he had had rudimentary plastic sugery carried out sometime before his death. A scar on the back of his thigh was what convinced her.

✝

In agreement with the FBI, Anna Sage had worn an orange outfit on the day of the shooting so that she would be recognized. Under the lights of the movie theater, it had looked red and she became known as "the lady in red." She would claim she did not know the man she was with was John Dillinger. The authorities failed to hold to their end of the bargain and in 1936 she was deported back to Romania where she lived until her death in 1947.

✝

Polly Hamilton worked as a waitress in Chicago and died in 1969. A month earlier, Evelyn "Billie" Frenchette, another of Dillinger's girlfriends, had also died. She had traveled with a crime-does-not pay carnival show when she had been released from prison.

✝

A third of the entire FBI budget for 1934 was used to bring down John Dillinger.

✝

"Baby Face" Nelson was shot dead by the FBI on November 27 that same year. Another infamous member of the gang, Homer Van Meter, died in a shoot-out with St. Paul police a month after Dillinger's killing.

✝

It was said, although never substantiated, that John Dillinger had an unusually large penis and that J. Edgar Hoover kept it in a jar. Hoover did keep several mementoes of Dillinger—his hat, spectacles, and change from his pocket—which he would proudly show off to visitors.

✠

"John Dillinger Day" is celebrated by the John Dillinger Died For You Society every year on July 22. They gather at the Biograph Theater and walk to the spot where he died, led by a bagpiper playing "Amazing Grace."

THE CONSPIRACY THEORY

Encouraged by the fact that, on seeing the body, Dillinger's father shouted out, "That's not my boy!" some people believed that it was not John Dillinger who died that evening. Many say that Hoover needed it to be Dillinger to save his job following several PR disasters.

There were said to be several inconsistencies:

* The body had brown eyes; Dillinger's were gray.
* The Colt pistol Dillinger was supposed to have been carrying at his death and which was put on display at FBI headquarters was actually manufactured five months after the gangster's death. If this is true, some claim, Dillinger was unarmed when he was shot.
* In 1963 a letter arrived at the *Indianapolis Star* containing a photograph of a man who looked like an older Dillinger.

F Scott Fitzgerald had been an alcoholic since college.
Although he wrote sober and claimed only to be a social
drinker, he was known to bribe waiters to bring him glasses of
straight gin masquerading as water. In addition to his alcoholism, he had suffered from tuberculosis on and off since 1919,
enduring a tubercular hemorrhage in 1929, and he was a victim
of depression resulting from his guilt over the incarceration of
his wife, Zelda, in a succession of hospitals and asylums.

The golden years of the Jazz Age, of which Fitzgerald was the
acknowledged chronicler, had long since passed. In 1920, at the
age of 24, he had achieved fame with the publication of his first
novel, *This Side of Paradise*, but he and Zelda, whom he married
shortly after the book's publication, lived opulently, consist-
ently spending more than they earned. Fitzgerald was forced to
write short stories for magazines such as *The Saturday Evening Post,
Collier's Weekly*, and *Esquire*. But even with the income from these
and the sale of movie rights for his books and short stories, he
was continually borrowing from his agent, Harold Ober, and
his editor at Scribner's, Maxwell Perkins, in order to pay Zelda's
medical bills and maintain his exuberant lifestyle.

Following a period of relentless financial stress, drunkenness,
and depression in the mid 1930s, described by him in his essay
"The Crack-Up," he found some relief, financially at least, in
Hollywood, working on commercial short stories and earning

$1,000 a week writing scripts for Metro-Goldwyn-Mayer. He also started his fifth and final novel, the ultimately unfinished *The Love of the Last Tycoon*, based on the life of film mogul Irving Thalberg. Estranged from Zelda, who would spend the rest of her life in institutions, he began a relationship with a nationally syndicated gossip columnist, English-born Sheila Graham. Graham had been engaged to the Marquess of Donegall, but had broken off the engagement within a month of meeting Fitzgerald.

Meanwhile his health continued to deteriorate. He was hospitalized in 1939, ostensibly for treatment for tuberculosis, but it has been speculated that he was actually being treated for his drinking.

Toward the end of November 1940, Fitzgerald had a serious heart attack in Schwab's drug store on Sunset Boulevard—an important meeting place for people in the movie industry. To aid his recovery, his doctor recommended he avoid strenuous exertion and suggested that he find an apartment on the ground floor to avoid stairs. Sheila Graham conveniently lived in a ground-floor apartment and he moved in with her. Fitzgerald was worried enough to stop drinking and took to his bed to work on *The Love of the Last Tycoon*.

On the night of December 20, he suffered a second heart attack and the next day, Sheila Graham found him on the floor of their living room. He suffered a third and fatal heart attack as he awaited a visit from his doctor. He was 44.

The Funeral

When she arrived at a memorial service at the Hollywood

funeral home in which Fitzgerald's body was kept before his funeral, writer Dorothy Chandler uttered, "The poor son of a bitch," a line spoken in *The Great Gatsby* by the philosopher Owl Eyes during a eulogy at the funeral of Jay Gatsby.

Fitzgerald's body was shipped to Rockville, Maryland, where Saint Mary's Catholic Church refused to allow him to be interred in the family plot because he had been a non-practicing Catholic at the time of his death. Consequently, he was buried at Rockville Union Cemetery in a funeral attended by only a handful of people.

In 1975, after a campaign waged by Scott and Zelda's daughter Scottie, the bodies of both Scott and Zelda were moved to Saint Mary's Church where today it is a much-visited part of the cemetery. Their tombstone bears the final words of *The Great Gatsby*: "So we beat on boats against the current, borne back ceaselessly into the past."

POST MORTEM

At the time of his death, none of Fitzgerald's books were in print. *The Love of the Last Tycoon*—originally known as *The Last Tycoon*—remained only half-written. It was edited by his friend Edmund Wilson and published in 1941 as *The Last Tycoon*. Despite being unfinished, it is regarded as a masterpiece.

Fitzgerald's heart condition cannot have been helped by his love of all things sweet—he loved Coca-Cola, poured huge amounts of sugar into his coffee, and was practically addicted to fudge.

✠

At his death, Fitzgerald's life and career were considered a warning to aspiring writers. In the opinion of most critics, he had failed to fulfill his genius. Typical of the reviews of his work was a headline over a review of *The Great Gatsby* when it was first published: F. SCOTT FITZGERALD'S LATEST DUD.

✠

The author Nathaniel West and his wife, Eileen McKenney, were killed in an automobile accident in El Centro, California, en route to Fitzgerald's memorial service in Los Angeles. Although it was common knowledge that West was an awful driver and many of his friends refused to get into a car with him, it is suggested that he was so grief-stricken by the death of his close friend that he ran a stop sign.

✠

Zelda began writing an unfinished novel of her own, *Caesar's Things*, after reading *The Love of the Last Tycoon*. She did not attend Scott's funeral and spent the next five years checking in and out of Highland Hospital in Ashville, North Carolina, where Scott had placed her in 1936. Her schizophrenia did not respond to treatment and on the night of March 10, 1948, she was one of nine women killed in a fire at the hospital.

✠

After the 1950s, Fitzgerald's oeuvre underwent a reappraisal. By 1960, *The Great Gatsby* was being recognized as the Great American Novel and Fitzgerald was acknowledged to be one of America's greatest writers.

CARY GRANT

I n 1986 the man christened Archibald Leach, but who had shot to fame as the debonair and handsome Cary Grant, was touring the States with his show, "A Conversation with Cary Grant," a lecture with film clips and a question-and-answer session. On the night of Friday, November 28, he arrived with his wife, Barbara Harris, at the Blackhawk Hotel in Davenport, Iowa. He was slated to do a show the following night at the Adler Theater.

On Saturday afternoon, Grant arrived at the theater for the 4 P.M. rehearsal for the evening's 8:30 performance. According to all present, he and his wife were in very good spirits and looked, as ever, great. Just before the rehearsal began, the event's sponsor remarked to the star, "I hope everything goes okay with the show," to which Grant replied morosely, "What happens, happens."

Perhaps he was right to be morose because what did happen was that he began to feel ill and vomited. He also complained of a severe headache. He was taken from the stage to his dressing room in a wheelchair and after some time eventually returned to his hotel, next door to the theater. Ever the trouper, he resisted suggestions that a doctor be called, worrying that the performance would have to be cancelled. But his condition deteriorated and there was no option but to cancel.

Eventually two doctors were called to examine him and at

9:15 P.M., he was taken by ambulance to St. Luke's Hospital. By the time the ambulance arrived at the hospital, however, he was in a coma and after 45 minutes of tests, he was rushed to intensive care.

On duty that night was cardiologist Dr. James Gilson, who assessed that Grant had had a massive stroke and concluded that there was little that could be done; his brain was badly damaged and he could no longer talk. One side of his body was completely paralyzed and his pupils were dilated. "Cary felt no pain," Dr. Gilson said, "and the family were very nice throughout the ordeal, and thanked me for all that was done."

At 11:22 P.M., Cary Grant died, age 82.

THE FUNERAL

At 3 A.M. the following morning, Barbara Harris accompanied her husband's body back to Los Angeles on a charter flight. On Sunday, November 30, his body was taken to Burbank where it was cremated by the Neptune Society, an organization founded to provide "a simple and dignified disposition of the decedent's remains at the time of death." In his will, Grant had stated, "I desire that my remains be cremated, and there be no formal services to note my passing." His ashes were handed over to his wife and Jennifer, the daughter from his marriage to actress Dyan Cannon.

POST MORTEM

After Grant's death the questions about whether he was gay or not arose again. To this day, they remain unanswered, although there has always been much speculation about his relationship with fellow actor Randolph Scott. The film director George Cukor, interviewed for the book *Hollywood Gays* said, "Oh, Cary won't talk about it. At most, he'll say they did some wonderful pictures together. But Randolph did admit it—to a friend, a male nurse (Scott was housebound in later years). He'd shown the nurse his scrapbook on Grant, and when the nurse asked him if it was true about their relationship, Randolph just smiled and nodded." However, Scott's son, interviewed for a BBC documentary about Cary Grant, claimed that his father and Cary never could have had an affair because his father's anus was checked when he was in the hospital, and "you can tell!"

EDWARD II

E dward II was never what you could call the most energetic of rulers. Son of Edward I and Eleanor of Castille, he was the first Prince of Wales and married Isabella, daughter of Philip IV of France. But he was never much interested in women and overindulged in everything—food, drink, and, especially, male favorites. He was detested by his barons and his people in equal measure.

Attempting to engage with an English king's customary passion for subduing the Scots, Edward was ignominiously defeated by Robert the Bruce at Bannockburn in 1314 and this was followed by risings in Ireland and Wales, eroding his authority still further.

He made a truce with Scotland for 13 years, but Charles IV of France, his wife's brother, seized his French territories. Edward sent his wife to negotiate with the French, but she hated her husband and his cronies as much as everyone else, and anyway, by this time she was having an affair with the disaffected noble Roger de Mortimer. Thus in 1326, Isabella returned to England, landing on the Suffolk coast with a large band of Edward's enemies.

Within a month of Isabella's landfall, Edward's government had collapsed. He fled the country only to be taken prisoner on November 16, 1326, in Southern Wales. From there he was taken to Kenilworth Castle and his young son, Edward III, replaced him on the throne, although Isabella and Roger de Mortimer were pulling the strings.

Having been moved to Berkeley Castle, there were several attempts to free him. In July 1327, one of these attempts succeeded but Edward was recaptured just over a month later and returned to Berkeley.

Eventually, Mortimer had had enough and he ordered the death of the former king.

A set of chronicles, known as *The Brut,* tell us that "when that night the king had gone to bed and was asleep, the traitors, against their homage and their fealty, went quietly into his chamber and laid a large table on his stomach and with other men's help pressed him down. At this he woke and in fear of his life, turned himself upside down. The tyrants, false traitors, then took a horn and put it into his fundament as deep as they could, and took a pit of burning copper, and put it through the horn into his body, and oftentimes rolled therewith his bowels, and so they killed their lord and nothing was perceived."

In other words, Edward II died the ignominious and horrific death of having red-hot molten copper poured into his rectum.

THE FUNERAL

Edward's body was placed in one coffin of lead inside another of wood and buried not at Westminster Cathedral, the traditional resting place of kings, but at Gloucester Cathedral.

POST MORTEM

Sir Thomas Gourney and William Ogle were accused of

Edward's murder but they escaped. There is no record of what became of Ogle, but Gurney was detained in Spain and is believed to have died while being brought back to England.

THE CONSPIRACY THEORY

Edward's half-brother, Edmund of Woodstock, believed that Edward was not killed and was, instead, being held at Corfe Castle. Apparently, this was the result of a campaign of disinformation by agents of Roger de Mortimer seeking to entrap him. (Successfully, as it turned out.)

Everyone seemed quite content to believe that Edward had indeed died until the publication of the Fieschi letter, or the "Confession of Edward II," in 1878. This consisted of a letter written by Manuele de Fieschi, the Bishop of Vicelli in Italy, to Edward III. Unknown for centuries, it was discovered by a Frenchman named Alexandre Germain as he was trawling through some ecclesiastical archives. The Fieschi letter claimed that Edward II was transferred from Berkeley Castle to Corfe Castle where he was held for 18 months before crossing into Ireland, where he remained for the next nine months. Then, disguised as a hermit, he returned to England and sailed to the continent, traveling across France to Avignon where he was received by the pope. After further travels he settled in Milan, which is where he came to the attention of Manuele de Fieschi.

ARCHDUKE FRANZ FERDINAND

Gavrilo Princip was born in what is now Bosnia, in 1894. The son of a postman, he had eight siblings, six of whom died in infancy, and from an early age he suffered from tuberculosis. In 1912, Princip traveled to Belgrade to continue his education, and in Serbia, joined the secret Serbian nationalist organization, the Black Hand. For the next two years most of his spare time was spent with other nationalists who favored a union between Bosnia and Serbia and independence from the Austro-Hungarian Empire.

It was announced that Archduke Franz Ferdinand, the heir to the throne of the Austro-Hungarian Empire, was going to visit Bosnia in June 1914 to tour the capital on the anniversary of the 1389 battle of Kosovo, a humiliating collective memory for all Serbs in which Serbia was defeated by the Turks, ending Serbia's independence as a nation. Dragutin Dimitrijević, the chief of the intelligence department in the Serbian army and head of the Black Hand, sent three men—Princip, Nedjelko Ćabrinović, and Trifko Grabež—to Sarajevo to assassinate the archduke; all three were tuberculosis sufferers and faced the prospect of an early death anyway.

Dimitrijević also considered Franz Ferdinand a serious threat to a union between Bosnia and Serbia. He was worried that Ferdinand's plans to grant concessions to the South Slavs would make an independent Serbian state more difficult to achieve.

The three assassins were each given a revolver, two bombs, and a small vial of cyanide. Like modern-day suicide bombers, they were to kill themselves after they had killed the archduke. Dimitrijević was, of course, especially keen that no one would be left alive to say who was behind the assassination.

Word got out about the plot, however, and Nikola Pašić, prime minister of Serbia, fearing that an assassination would lead to war with Austro-Hungary, issued orders for the men's arrest when they left the country. But the orders were never implemented and Princip, Čabrinović and Grabež made it to Bosnia where they joined up with a number of other conspirators.

On Sunday, June 28, Franz Ferdinand and his pregnant wife, Princess Sophie von Chotkovato, arrived by train at Sarajevo Station, from where they were taken to the city hall for a reception hosted by General Oskar Potiorek, governor of Bosnia. The mayor of Sarajevo and the city's commissioner of police rode in the first car and in the second, the top rolled back to let the crowd see the royal couple, were the archduke and his wife, accompanied by Potiorek and Count von Harrach.

The seven members of the Black Hand spaced themselves out along the route, each with orders to take action as the car passed. Another assassin for the the Black Hand, anarchist Muhamed Mehmedbašić, was the first to see the car. However, he took fright and the motorcade passed unharmed. He later claimed that there had been a policeman nearby and he feared he would be arrested before he had a chance to throw his bomb. Čabrinović was next and he kept his nerve, stepping out of the crowd at 10:15 A.M. and launching his bomb at the royal car. Seeing the bomb, Sophie ducked, and Franz Ferdinand deflected it with his arm, causing it to bounce off the back of the vehicle and explode under the car behind them, seriously injuring Eric von Merizzi and Count Boos-Waldeck, two of the car's occupants, as well as a number of spectators. Franz Urban, the archduke's driver, accelerated and the archduke's car sped through the streets of Sarajevo to the city hall, making it impossible for any of the other conspirators to carry out their plans.

Following his orders to the letter, Čabrinović swallowed his cyanide and jumped into the Miljacka River, pursued by several men, including two detectives. Unfortunately for him, however, the poison did not work and he was apprehended and taken to the nearest police station.

In spite of all this, the reception went ahead as planned and when it was over Franz Ferdinand insisted on being taken to the hospital to visit those who had been injured in the attack. When it was suggested that this might be dangerous, Oskar Potiorek replied, "Do you think Sarajevo is full of assassins?"

Nevertheless, Potiorek *did* conclude that the city center would be dangerous and devised a route straight along the Appel Quay to the hospital. Unfortunately, he forgot to tell Franz Urban, and the royal driver turned right on to Franz Joseph Street, where Gavril Princip just happened to be standing on the corner. Realizing that the driver had taken a wrong turn, Potiorek shouted at him. Urban stopped the car and began to reverse, moving slowly past Princip, who stepped forward, drew his gun, and from a distance of about six and a half feet, fired several shots into the car, hitting the archduke in the neck and Sophie in the abdomen.

Franz Ferdinand had been hit in the jugular vein, and as Count von Harrach, traveling in the car with them, took out his handkerchief to wipe away the blood from the archduke's lips, Sophie cried out, "For God's sake! What happened to you?" Then she sank down with her face between the archduke's knees. She had fainted from shock. The archduke said, "Sophie, Sophie, don't die. Live for my children." Von Harrach seized the archduke by the coat collar to prevent his head from sinking forward and asked him if he was in great pain. Franz Ferdinand clearly answered, "It is nothing," his face slightly distorted. He then repeated this six or seven times, every time drifting closer to unconsciousness as his voice faded. Then there was a brief pause followed by a convulsive rattle in his throat.

The car sped off to the governor's residence at Konak, but the royal pair died soon after they arrived.

THE FUNERAL

Franz Ferdinand and Princess Sophie were given a joint funeral mass, but her plinth was placed 18 inches lower than his, evidence of lingering antagonism from his family toward her due to the fact that she was not a member of one of the reigning European dynasties. They were buried in the crypt of their country home, Schloss Artstetten.

POST MORTEM

Following his orders after shooting Franz Ferdinand and

Sophie von Chotkovato, Princip turned his gun on himself, but a man behind him saw what he was doing, and seized his right arm. A couple of policeman joined the struggle and Princip was arrested.

✠

Princip and Nedjelko Ćabrinović were both interrogated by the police, eventually giving the names of their fellow conspirators. Muhamed Mehmedbašić managed to escape to Serbia but Trifko Grabež, Danilo Ilić, Vaso Cubrilović, Cvijetko Popović, Misko Jovanović, and Veljko Ćubrilovic were arrested and charged with treason and murder.

✠

The eight men were found guilty. Under Austro-Hungarian law, capital punishment could not be imposed on someone who was under the age of twenty. Princip, 19 years and 11 months at the time of the assassination, consequently received the maximum penalty of twenty years.

✠

Princip's only sign of regret was the statement that he was sorry he had killed the wife of the archduke. He had aimed only at her husband and would have preferred that the other bullet should have struck General Potiorek.

✠

Nedjelko Ćabrinović's statement in court said, "We thought that only people of noble character were capable of committing political assassinations. We heard it said that he [Archduke Franz Ferdinand] was an enemy of the Slavs. Nobody directly told us 'kill him'; but in this environment, we arrived at the idea ourselves. I would like to add something else. Although Princip is playing the hero, and although we all wanted to appear as heroes, we still have profound regrets. In the first place, we did not know that the late Franz Ferdinand was a father. We were greatly touched by the words he addressed to his wife: 'Sophie, stay alive for our children.' We are anything you want, except criminals. In my name and in the name of my comrades, I ask the children of the late successor to the throne to forgive us. As for you, punish us according to your understanding. We are not criminals. We are honest people, animated by noble sentiments; we are idealists; we wanted to do good; we have loved our people; and we shall die for our ideals."

✠

Austrian reaction to the assassination was swift, as the Sarajevo crisis was seen as the empire's last chance to assert its supremacy in the Balkans. Austrian Foreign Minister Count Leopold von Berchtold was determined to make use of the assassinations to crush once and for all the Serbian nationalist movement. He sent an envoy to Berlin, which was assured by Emperor William II that Germany would fully support any action the dual monarchy might take against Serbia. On July 6, German Chancellor Theobald von Bethmann-Hollweg issued the blank check of unconditional German support.

✠

On July 23, 1914, Austria-Hungary presented Serbia with a lengthy list of demands, with a 48 hour period in which to comply. These demands included abolishing all Pan-Serb propaganda, expelling from office any persons thought to have nationalist sympathies, taking legal action against certain officials designated by Austria-Hungary, and allowing agents of the Dual Monarchy to control all investigations and proceedings concerning the Sarajevo murders. Minutes before the July 25 deadline, Serbia issued a conciliatory reply to von Berchtold's demands, stating that Serbia wished the dispute to be submitted to the International Tribunal at The Hague. This conciliation was rejected. On July 28, 1914, Austria-Hungary declared war on Serbia. World War I had begun.

Gavrilo Princip's tuberculosis finally killed him on April 28, 1918, shortly before the end of the war his actions had precipitated.

MAHATMA GANDHI

O n Friday, January 30, 1948, the 78-year-old Mahatma Gandhi woke punctually, as always, at half past three in the morning. It was just 12 days since his successful fast to bring about a rapprochement between Hindus and Muslims in Delhi. But ten days previous, there had been an attempt on his life when a bomb exploded a short distance from where he was addressing a prayer meeting. As he opened his eyes that morning, he knew his life was in danger.

Rising from the wooden plank on which he slept, Gandhi woke his attendant Brij Krishna Chandiwala and his grandnieces, Manu and Abha. They said prayers and then Manu and Abha, whom he called his walking sticks, helped him walk into the inner room where his legs were covered with a blanket. The sun had not yet risen as he worked on the draft of a proposal for a new constitution for his party written the previous night for the forthcoming Congress Working Committee meeting. It would become known as Gandhi's "Last Will and Testament for the Nation." At 4:45 A.M. he drank a glass of lemon, honey, and hot water and one hour later, his daily glass of orange juice.

Gandhi was still weak from his fast and he slept for thirty minutes. A little later, he had his first meeting of the day while taking his morning constitutional in his room. Then he left to have a massage, handing his draft for the new constitution to his secretary Pyarelal and asking him to "Fill in any gaps."

Brij Krishna gave Gandhi a half-hour massage in a room next door to his sitting room, with two electric heaters warming the cold morning air. Lying on the table, the Mahatma read the morning papers. Manu then gave him his bath after which he was weighed. He weighed 109 1/2 pounds. He had put on two and a half pounds since ending the fast.

At 9:30 A.M., Gandhi had his breakfast—cooked vegetables, 12 ounces of goat's milk, four tomatoes, four oranges, carrot juice, and a decoction of ginger, sour limes, and aloes. He talked with his secretary and told him that he planned to go to Pakistan. An old friend from his South African days, Rustom Sorabji, then paid a visit with his family.

At 10:30 A.M., Gandhi again slept and the soles of his feet were rubbed with ghee. Waking at midday, he drank some hot water and honey and then walked unaided to the bathroom, the first time since his fast that he had done so.

He welcomed a delegation of Delhi Muslim leaders and after more meetings, he lay down in the sunshine and had an abdominal mud pack applied, wearing a peasant's bamboo hat while Kanu and Abha again pressed his feet. When told that the papers were saying that he was leaving for Sevagram, his ashram, on the first of the month, Gandhi replied mischievously, "Yes, the papers have announced that Gandhi would be going on the first, but who that Gandhi is, I do not know."

At around 1:30 P.M., he drank a few ounces of carrot and lemon juice and met some blind and homeless refugees. Then at 2:15 P.M., the daily round of interviews began. Representatives from India and beyond sought audiences with him and he did not finish his last interview until 4 P.M.

Another meeting followed, and while talking, Gandhi ate his evening meal—goat's milk, vegetable soup, oranges, and carrot juice. He then asked for his charkar or spinning wheel. The spinning wheel was a powerful symbol for Gandhi. For him it represented a technology that was simple and could be used by everyone.

Five o'clock was the customary time for prayers, but Gandhi was already ten minutes late on this occasion, having forgotten to put on the Ingersoll watch he normally wore. He was told the time and reluctantly got up, put on his sandals, and went through the side door out into the twilight. He was wearing a shawl and was leaning on Manu on his right and Abha on his left. Manu carried his spittoon, glasses case, and rosary, as well as her notebook. Brij Krishna walked behind them with members of the Birla family, the owners of the house, and some others.

Since the failed assassination attempt a few weeks previously, about thirty policemen, uniformed and plainclothes, were stationed around Birla House, but today the Mahatma's personal plainclothes policeman, A.N. Bhatia, was absent, having been reassigned elsewhere.

As he was late, Gandhi did not follow his usual route through the leafy arbor to the right side of the grounds. Instead, he took a shortcut across the lawn to the steps that led to the terrace where prayers were held. His mood was light. He joked about the raw carrot Abha had given him that day, calling it cattle food. She replied that Ba, Gandhi's deceased wife, used to call it horse food. As they hurried along, Gandhi replied, "Is it not grand of me to relish what no one else would care for?"

At the top of the steps, the Mahatma brought his palms together in greeting. The hushed crowd, several hundred strong, parted to make a passage for him to the wooden platform. Critically, no one walked in front of Gandhi.

The Mahatma had taken just a few paces from the steps when Nathuram Godse, a member of the right-wing political organization Hindu Mahasabha, whose members deeply resented what they saw as Gandhi's appeasement of India's Muslims, pushed his way through the crowd and approached Gandhi with his palms joined. A tiny black Beretta pistol was hidden between them, easily smuggled in as Gandhi did not allow the police to search people entering the grounds of Birla House for the prayer meetings. Godse bowed low and said, "*Namaste*, Gandhiji," and Gandhi acknowledged him, joining his palms together. Manu thought Godse was going to kiss the Mahatma's feet, something that she knew the holy man did not like. So she motioned him away. "Brother, Bapu is already late for prayers," she said, "why are you bothering him?"

Godse pushed her aside with his left hand, the gun in his right hand momentarily exposed. She dropped the glasses case and the other things she was carrying and for several moments she carried on arguing with the assailant, but when the rosary fell to the ground, she bent down to retrieve it. At this moment, Godse pulled the trigger and fired three bullets into Gandhi's abdomen and chest at almost point-blank range. Gandhi remained standing, his palms still together in greeting. Then he was heard to gasp, "*He Ram, He Ram*," ("Oh God, oh God"). He slowly sank to the ground, palms still joined. The air was filled with gun smoke and confusion and panic reigned.

The Mahatma was now slumped on the ground, his head resting in his nieces' laps. His face had turned deathly white, while his white Australian wool shawl turned red with the little man's blood. Within seconds Mahatma Gandhi was dead. It was 5:17 P.M.

THE FUNERAL

On February 12, 1948, almost a million people accompanied Mahatma Gandhi's funeral procession to the cremation grounds by the holy waters of the Yamuna, near New Delhi.

A funeral pyre of stone, brick, and earth had been built at Rajghat, close to the river, eight feet square and two feet high. Long thin sandalwood logs, sprinkled with incense, were stacked on it. The Mahatma's body was placed on it with his head to the north and at 4:45 P.M., Ramdas, Gandhi's third son, set the pyre alight, accompanied by a huge groan from the crowd. Ramdas then consigned the ashes to the Ganges.

Later, in similar ceremonies at sacred sites along rivers and seashores at some fifty places in India and Pakistan, portions of Gandhi's ashes were ceremoniously committed to the waters in the presence of millions of mourners. Millions more, in towns and villages with community wireless sets, listened to a three-hour commentary on the Allahabad ceremony, broadcast in English and Hindu by All-India Radio. All work throughout the country stopped that day, the last of a 13-day period of state mourning.

POST MORTEM

The film *Gandhi*, directed by Richard Attenborough and
starring Sir Ben Kingsley in an the uncanny re-creation of the
Mahatma, is judged to be one of the greatest biopics ever made.
For Gandhi's funeral, which begins the film, Attenborough
hoped for a mostly unpaid crowd of 150,000 people. On the
day, an extra quarter of a million turned up, making it easily the
biggest crowd ever to appear in a film.

Che Guevara and his men—consisting of Cubans, Argentineans, Peruvians, and Bolivians—had been attacking the Bolivian army with considerable success since spring 1967. At the end of August, however, the army had retaliated with a significant victory, wiping out a third of Che's men. To make matters worse, the guerrilla leader's health was beginning to fail.

Two years earlier he had suddenly resigned from his positions as president of Cuba's national bank and as Minister of Industry and had said farewell to the Cuban Revolution he had created with his brother-in-arms, Fidel Castro. He wanted to export revolution to Latin America and Africa and in pursuit of this ambition, he left Cuba to set up guerrilla forces firstly in the Congo and then in Bolivia.

But by September 29, Che and a group of 17 men were trapped in Valle Serrano, in the jungles of southeast Bolivia, and the second Ranger Battalion of the Bolivian army was ordered into the area to deal with them. This force of one thousand three hundred men had been trained and equipped by U.S. Special Forces, or "Green Berets," and was being directed by the CIA, with one aim and one aim only—the capture of Che Guevara.

On October 8, in Quebrada del Yuro, at around 1:30 P.M., Che's final battle began.

The army had received word that guerrillas were located in the Churro Ravine and, on entering the area, they immediately bumped into a group of them. Che and a colleague, Simeon Cuba "Willy" Sarabia, a former Bolivian tin miner, tried to break out, but a machine-gun crew caught sight of them and opened fire, hitting Che in the leg several times. He was helped by Willy in the direction of the Tuscal Ravine where the two men rested for a few minutes. They then moved north, but it was directly into the line of fire of some government soldiers. A gunfight erupted and Che was hit again in the right leg. His gun was knocked out of his hand as another bullet pierced his right forearm. As soldiers approached, he was heard to shout, "Don't shoot! I'm Che Guevara and I am worth more to you alive than dead." By 3:30 P.M., the battle was over and Che and Willy had been taken prisoner.

They were brought before Captain Prado, who was directing the operation and who immediately ordered his radio operator to signal the divisional headquarters in Vallegrande to give them the news that Che had at last been captured. The coded message read: "Hello Saturno, we have Papá!" (Saturno was the code for Colonel Joaquin Zenteno, commandant of the eighth Bolivian Army Division, and "Papá" the code for Che.) The incredulous colonel asked Prado to confirm the message and on receipt of this confirmation, celebrations erupted among the divisional headquarters staff. Zenteno radioed Prado and told him to immediately transfer Che and any other prisoners to the nearby village of La Higuera.

Che was carried on a blanket by four soldiers to La Higuera, about four miles away, arriving at their destination not long after dark. He and Willy were put into the village's one-room schoolhouse.

At 6:15 A.M., CIA operative Félix Rodríguez—later involved in the Iran-Contra scandal and nowadays a close friend of the Bush family—arrived by helicopter, along with Colonel Zenteno. He described the scene in the schoolhouse as "gruesome." Che was lying in dirt, his arms bound behind his back and his feet tied together, next to the bodies of the other guerrillas who had been taken. According to Rodríguez, he looked "like a piece of trash," with his clothing torn to shreds and his hair matted. Later Rodríguez recalled the scene: "I had mixed emotions when I first arrived there. Here was the man who had assassinated many of my countrymen. And nevertheless, when I saw him, the way he looked . . . I felt really sorry for him."

Rodríguez set up a radio and transmitted a coded message to a South American CIA station that was retransmitted to the CIA headquarters in Langley, Virginia. After he photographed Che's diary and other secured documents, he talked with Che and had his picture taken with him. He took the guerilla's wristwatch as a souvenir.

By 10 A.M., the Bolivian officers were confronted with the dilemma of what to do with the revolutionary. He could not be prosecuted because a trial would focus world attention on him and could conceivably create sympathetic propaganda for him and for Cuba. Consequently, the decision was made to execute him immediately. The official story would report that he died in battle.

Rodríguez received a call from superior command at Vallegrande and was ordered to conduct Operation Five Hundred and Six Hundred. "Five Hundred" was the Bolivian code for Che and "Six Hundred" was the order to kill him. He informed Colonel Zenteno of the order, but also told him that the U.S. government had instructed *him* to keep Che alive at all costs. The CIA and the U.S. government had arranged helicopters and airplanes to take him to Panama for interrogation. But Zenteno said he must obey his own orders and Rodríguez decided "to let history take its course," as he later put it.

He entered the schoolhouse to tell Che of the orders from Bolivian high command. Che admitted, "It is better like this. I should never have been captured alive." He gave Rodríguez a message for his wife and one for Castro. The two men embraced and Rodríguez left the room.

A captain by the name of Perez entered the schoolhouse and asked Che if he wanted anything before he died. Che replied that he only wanted to "die with a full stomach." When Perez sneeringly asked him if he was "materialist," Che replied, as he had to most of the questions the Bolivians had asked him, "Perhaps." Perez called him a "poor shit" and left.

No one among the noncommissioned officers wanted to carry out the order and straws had to be drawn. Sergeant Jaime Teran pulled the shortest one and went to the schoolhouse where he found Che leaning against the wall. He asked to be allowed to stand up for his execution. "I know what you have come for and I am ready," the guerilla said. Teran was terrified, however, and fled the building, only to be ordered immediately to return by his senior officers.

When Teran came back into the hut, Che said he would remain standing. Teran angrily told him to sit down, but Che retorted, "I know you have come to kill me. Shoot, you are only going to kill a man." These were the last words Che Guevara spoke.

Teran, averting his gaze from the guerrilla leader's face, shot him in the arms and legs and then in the chest. Other soldiers came into the schoolhouse at that point and took their turn at shooting into the corpse of the legendary revolutionary.

POST MORTEM

Following the execution, Che's body was exhibited for 24 hours before disappearing. The authorities were afraid of creating a place of pilgrimage for his sympathizers.

✠

His hands were amputated and preserved in formaldehyde as evidence that he was dead.

✠

Two doctors at the hospital in Vallegrande, Bolivia, signed a death certificate that stated: "On October 9 at 5:30 P.M., there arrived Ernesto Guevara Lynch, approximately forty years of age, the cause of death being multiple bullet wounds in the thorax and extremities. Preservative was applied to the body." On the same day, an autopsy report recorded the multiple bullets wounds found in Che's body. "The cause of death," stated the autopsy report, "was the thorax wounds and consequent hemorrhaging."

✠

On October 14, students at Central University of Venezuela protested at the U.S. involvement in Che's death. Demonstrations were organized outside the American embassy, American businesses, and the homes of U.S. ex-pats.

✠

On October 15, Bolivian President Barrientos claimed that Che had been cremated and his ashes were buried in a hidden place somewhere in the Vallegrande region.

✠

On October 16, the Bolivian armed forces released a communiqué on the death of Che Guevara. The communiqué was "based on documents released by the Military High Command on October 9 concerning the combat that took place at La Higuera between units of the armed forces and the red group commanded by Ernesto 'Che' Guevara, as a result of which he, among others, lost his life." The report stated that Guevara died "more or less at 8 P.M. on Sunday, October 8 as a result of his wounds."

✠

On October 18, Fidel Castro delivered a eulogy for Che Guevara to nearly a million people—one of his largest audiences ever—in Havana's Plaza de la Revolución. Castro proclaimed that Che's lifelong struggle against imperialism and his ideals would be the inspiration for future generations of revolutionaries. His life was a "glorious page of history" because of his extraordinary military accomplishments and his unequaled combination of virtues that made him an "artist in guerrilla warfare." Castro professed that Che's murderers would be disappointed when they realized that "the art to which he dedicated his life and intelligence cannot die."

In 1995, Mario Vargas Salinas, a soldier who had taken part in the secret burial of Che, said that the revolutionary and his comrades had been buried in a pit dug by a bulldozer near Vallegrande's airstrip. He was unable, however, to recall the precise location. In 1997 aerial technology was used to find areas in the earth where the ground had been disturbed. A trough was dug and human remains were found. One of the skeletons had no hands and was covered by a military jacket. It was Che Guevara.

On July 13, 1997, a ceremony in Havana, attended by Fidel Castro and other Cuban officials, marked the return of Che's remains to Cuba.

On October 17, 1997, at a ceremony attended by Castro and thousands of Cubans, Che was reburied in Santa Clara, Cuba. In the small town where Che's remains were found, the people who knew the revolutionary now talk about him not as a human, but as a "brujo"—a sorcerer. They say it doesn't matter that his remains have been found. He is still alive in spirit form.

George Harrison had always been a heavy smoker, the Beatles's love for "ciggies" being well-known from their earliest days. In 1998 he was diagnosed with throat cancer but overcame it. Not long after, however, he developed lung cancer and he soon knew that it would prove fatal. He contacted Gavin de Becker—the guru of celebrity security—during his stay at Staten Island University Hospital where he was registered under the name Arias and was receiving last-chance cancer treatment, to arrange a secretive funeral.

Around this time, ten days before his death, he was visited by fellow ex-Beatle Paul McCartney. McCartney has described how they held hands and laughed and joked together. George was adamant that he would not die in a hospital and Paul offered his Beverly Hills mansion, formerly owned by Kurt Cobain's widow, Courtney Love. So the dying guitarist travelled to UCLA Medical Center for drugs and pain management before heading to Paul's house to die.

For 36 hours George drifted in and out of consciousness, his wife, Olivia, and son, Dhani, at his bedside. George's old friend, the sitar player Ravi Shankar, was present and played throughout the vigil. Pictures of the Hindu gods Krishna and Rama were placed at the bedside and two of George's friends from the Krishna faith, Shayam Sundara and Mukunda, chanted quietly. The 58-year-old ex-Beatle is reported to have passed away "serenely."

The Funeral

George's body was wrapped in a shawl and covered with holy oils. An unmarked white van from Hollywood Forever Cemetery arrived to collect the body. The funeral attendants briefly joined hands with the Harrison family and the security staff and said a small prayer. The van stopped briefly at the doctor's for the death certificate to be signed and then took him to the cemetery crematorium, where he was cremated in a cardboard casket in a Krishna service.

On the following Monday his ashes arrived in India where they were scattered in Allahabad where the three holiest rivers in Hinduism converge—the Ganges, the Yamuna, and the legendary Saraswati.

Post Mortem

The Harrison family released the following statement: "We are deeply touched by the outpouring of love and compassion from people around the world. The profound beauty of the moment of George's passing—of his awakening from this dream—was no surprise to those of us who knew how he longed to be with God. In that pursuit, he was relentless."

✠

The world was invited to join Olivia and Dhani in a minute of meditation on the following Monday at 1:30 P.M.

✠

George was survived by his siblings Harry, Peter, and Louise, as well as by his first wife, Pattie Boyd, whom he had met on the set of the Beatles' first film, *A Hard Day's Night*, in 1964.

According to press reports and many of the obituaries, George died in the home of his friend, Gavin de Becker. His death certificate describes the "place of death" as an address in Coldwater Canyon, Beverly Hills. However, the Coldwater Canyon address is nonexistent. Paul McCartney's house is accepted to be the most likely place of death. It is thought that the ex-Beatle tried to create a smokescreen so that the property in which he died would not become a stop on Hollywood's ghoulish death tours—or featured in books such as this.

BUDDY HOLLY

It was a time of change for Buddy Holly. He had broken up his backup group, the Crickets, and had left his record company. Recently married and with a child on the way, he badly needed the money that touring provided and so he set out on the "Winter Dance Party" tour, a grueling procession of one-night stands across the Midwest in the middle of winter. Worse still, the tour bus was unheated and kept breaking down. It was so bad that the drummer, Carl Brunch, suffered from frostbite.

Headlining the tour were Holly, Richie Valens, and J.P. Richardson—the Big Bopper—and also on the bus were former Cricket Tommy Allsup, a longtime friend of Holly's from his hometown of Lubbock, Texas, Waylon Jennings, and singing group Dion and the Belmonts.

By February 2, 1959, when they played the Surf Ballroom in Clear Lake, Iowa, both Valens and the Big Bopper were suffering from colds and Holly could not face the bus journey to their next gig in Moorhead, Minnesota, a journey of several hundred miles. He arranged the charter of a plane to Fargo, North Dakota, from where it was a short journey to Moorhead. The cost was $108 and Holly offered the two remaining seats to anyone in the party who was willing to cough up the required $36 each to cover the cost. Waylon Jennings wanted to fly but gave up his seat to the ailing Big Bopper. Tommy Allsup was also going to fly, but lost his seat on the toss of a coin to Richie Valens. Holly then used a pay phone in the lobby of the ballroom to call his wife and Valens phoned his brother, both complaining bitterly about the conditions they had to endure on the tour.

As they were leaving, Holly teased Waylon Jennings about the bus. "You're not going on that plane tonight?" he joked. Jennings replied that he was going to be on the bus and Holly retorted, "Well, I hope your old bus freezes up again!" Jennings shot back, "Well, I hope your old plane crashes!" They both got their wishes that night.

The plane was a small four-passenger Beechcraft Bonanza, named *American Pie*. It was painted red with a black trim and its pilot, 21-year-old Roger Peterson, was inexperienced and unqualified to fly in such difficult conditions.

As the party made its way from Clear Lake to Mason City Airport the weather was fine, but a weather warning had been issued by the National Weather Service, a warning not received by either Peterson or by Jerry Dwyer who owned the Dwyer Flying Service from which the plane was being chartered.

The plane took off at around one in the morning into a blinding snowstorm. It came down in a cornfield belonging to Albert Juhl, only 15 miles northwest of Mason City. All on board were killed instantly.

THE FUNERAL

The Big Bopper's wake was held in the Broussard's Funeral Home, in Beaumont, Texas, and he was buried in Beaumont.

Private Elvis Presley and Colonel Tom Parker sent yellow roses to his funeral.

On Saturday, February 7, Ritchie Valens's body was taken from the Noble Chapel Funeral Home in the San Fernando Valley, to San Fernando Mission Cemetery. His body was driven in a copper-colored hearse.

Buddy Holly was also buried on February 7. Services were held in Lubbock, Texas, at the Tabernacle Baptist Church. Over a thousand mourners attended the service, but his pregnant widow did not.

POST MORTEM

When Jerry Dwyer did not receive news of the safe landing of the plane in Fargo, North Dakota, he became concerned and decided to mount a search. The next morning was foggy. This prevented him from flying until about 9 A.M. He finally took off along the same flight path as the *American Pie* and found the wreckage within five minutes. It had gone unnoticed for eight hours along a fence in that snow-covered field, about a quarter mile from the nearest country road.

✠

Holly had $193 on him when his body was found in the wreckage. The Mason City coroner is reported to have taken $11.65 of it, for his fees.

✠

The "Winter Dance Party" tour continued. The relatively unknown singers Bobby Vee, Paul Anka, and Fabian were drafted to replace Holly, Valens, and the Big Bopper.

The crash site became a tourist attraction and some of the visitors to Albert Juhl's field were given souvenir pieces of the wreckage.

Holly's wife lost the baby she had been expecting. Many years later, Tommy Alsup opened a club which he called The Head's Up Saloon to commemorate the coin toss that saved his life.

In 1972 Don McLean had a worldwide hit with the song "American Pie" which was dedicated to the victims of the crash and memorably described that incident as "The day the music died." It was later rerecorded by Madonna.

In 1980, Holly's glasses, four dice, and the Big Bopper's watch were discovered in an envelope in the county courthouse at Mason City. These items were returned to the families.

In 1990, Gary Busey, who played Buddy Holly in the film *The Buddy Holly Story*, bought one of Holly's guitars at an auction in New York. He is said to have paid $242,000 for it. The Rock and Roll Hall of Fame bought a pair of his glasses for $25,000. In 1976, ex-Beatle Paul McCartney bought the rights to all of Buddy Holly's songs.

October 1926 was not the best month of Harry Houdini's life. For starters, on the night of October 11, during a performance of his famous Underwater Torture escape, a chain slipped, fracturing his ankle. Houdini characteristically refused the advice of a doctor who was in the audience and stubbornly persevered with his performance, hopping painfully from stunt to stunt on his one good leg and requiring the help of his assistants to finish his tricks. He then ignored doctor's orders that he should rest the leg for two weeks and stubbornly carried on with his tour. During the next two days, he performed in agony, wearing a splint and a leg brace.

Things got even worse 11 days later when, lying on a couch in his dressing room in the Princess Theater in Montreal and opening his mail, Houdini welcomed two students from McGill University who had heard him deliver a lecture the previous week. Preoccupied with his letters, the magician was not paying much attention when one of the boys, J. Gordon Whitehead, a tough six-footer, questioned him about his ability to take powerful blows to the stomach. Still reading his mail, Houdini began to say to the boy that he could indeed withstand blows, but he had to brace himself in anticipation of the punch. However, as he stood to prepare himself, the student leaned forward and, without warning, punched Houdini hard three times in the abdomen. When Whitehead saw the startled look in the magician's eyes, he was shocked, explaining that he thought he had been given permission to throw the punch. Houdini, in considerable pain, recovered sufficiently to reassure White and to go onstage for his performance.

Throughout the show, however, it was evident that Houdini was suffering and later that night he admitted to crippling abdominal pain. Arriving for his next engagement in Detroit, he was examined by doctors who diagnosed his pain as a symptom of acute appendicitis. But, even though his temperature had now risen to 102 degrees, he still refused to go to the hospital, insisting that the show must go on.

Houdini made it through the Detroit performance despite his soaring temperature, severe abdominal pains, and continuing discomfort from his broken ankle. He missed cues and once again his assistants were often called upon to complete tricks for him. At the interval, ice packs were put on him to try to ease his fever. Just before the third act, however, he turned to his chief assistant, James Collins, and whispered, "Drop the curtain, Collins, I can't go any further."

As soon as the curtain dropped, Houdini fell to the stage. He was immediately helped to his dressing room and changed out of his stage clothes, but still refused to go to the hospital for treatment, returning instead to his hotel.

Early next morning, October 25, the illusionist was still in agony and his wife, Bess, insisted on a doctor being called. The hotel physician attended and immediately called a surgeon, but Houdini would still not go to the hospital until he had spoken to his own personal physician in New York, Dr. William Stone.

Stone advised him to listen to what the doctor was saying and Houdini was at last rushed to Grace Hospital where an operation was performed immediately. It was discovered that his appendix had ruptured, causing peritonitis, and the doctors informed a shocked Bess that it was unlikely that her husband would survive. They gave him an experimental serum and operated again on October 29, but by this time the sepsis had spread through his system.

Houdini was a tough man and hung on until the early morning of October 31—Halloween—when, in the darkness of his hospital room, he turned to Bess and his brother Hardeen, who were at his bedside, and whispered, "I'm getting tired and I can't fight any more." He turned his head away and died, 52 years old.

THE FUNERAL

Houdini's body was taken to the funeral home of W.R. Hamilton and Company in a bronze, silk-lined coffin with a full-length glass top. He had built it himself just four weeks before his death, specifically to use in his act.

A special Pullman car was attached to a train called *Detroiter,* to take him from Michigan Central Station on the night of Monday, November 1. Bess Houdini, in shock since her husband's death, arrived in a wheelchair, and in the private car carrying the Houdini party were Houdini's brothers, Theodore Hardeen and Nathan J. Weiss; Miss Julia Sawyer, a niece; Miss Julia Karchere, a cousin of Mrs. Houdini; H. Elliot Stuckel, Houdini's manager, and James Collins, his technical director.

Houdini was buried on November 4, in Machpélah Cemetery in Ferndale, Michigan, next to the grave of his mother. Two thousand people attended his funeral and, at his request, he was buried with a collection of his mother's letters beneath the pillow on which his head rested.

POST MORTEM

It is now thought that Houdini was already suffering from appendicitis when Whitehead punched him. It is likely, however, that he believed his stomach pains were a result of the punches and not appendicitis.

In the days following his death, there were reports from clairvoyants worldwide who claimed to have predicted that he would die. Among them was his former friend, Sir Arthur Conan Doyle, with whom he had had a very public disagreement about spiritualism. Conan Doyle's circle had recorded a message about Houdini several months before his death. The message is reported to have said: "Houdini is doomed, doomed, doomed!"

Houdini's friend and fellow magician Joseph Dunninger said that on one early morning in October 1926, Houdini called him in New York and asked him to drive over to his house on West 113th Street, as he had to move some things. When the car was loaded, he asked Dunninger to drive through the park. Dunninger said that as they got to the exit on Central Park West, near 72nd Street, Houdini grabbed him by the arm and urged him to go back to his house. When Dunninger asked him if he had forgotten something, Houdini said, "Don't ask questions, Joe, just turn around and go back." Arriving at the house, Houdini climbed out of the car and stood looking at it in the rain. He stayed that way for a few minutes and then he got back into the car without saying a word. Dunninger drove off and when the two men again approached the western exit of the park, he glanced over and saw that Houdini's shoulders had started to shake. He was crying. When Dunninger asked him what was wrong Houdini replied, "I've seen my house for the last time, Joe. I'll never see my house again."

To Dunninger's knowledge, he never did.

✠

Bess began efforts to honor her husband's requests about attempting contact with him after his death. Every Sunday at the hour of his death, she would shut herself in a room with his photograph and wait for a sign. She made no secret of the fact that she was waiting for a secret, coded message from Houdini, and word spread that she had offered $10,000 to any medium who could deliver a true message from the dead illusionist. Every week a new medium would emerge claiming to have broken the code, but no one did until 1928, when the well-known medium Arthur Ford announced that he had a message for Beth. He said it was from Houdini's mother and consisted of just one word—"forgive." Bess informed the world that this was the first message she had received that "had any appearance of truth." That November, Ford received another message, this time from Houdini himself. It was a coded message—

"Rosabelle, answer, tell, pray, answer, look, tell, answer, answer, tell." It emerged that "Rosabelle" was the title of a song that had been popular when Bess had first met Houdini. The rest of the message was a series of code words spelling out the word "believe." However, there were accusations that Ford was a fraud, especially as it emerged that the code had been included in a book published in 1927.

✠

Bess Houdini persevered with what became known as the Houdini Séances. Ten years after his death, the final one on the roof of the Knickerbocker Hotel in Hollywood was featured in a worldwide radio broadcast. However, despite their entreaties to the dead magician to lift the table or do something to communicate with them, nothing happened. At the end, a disappointed Bess told the world, "Houdini did not come through. My last hope is gone. I do not believe that Houdini can come back to me—or to anyone. The Houdini shrine has burned for ten years. I now, reverently, turn out the light. It is finished. Good night, Harry!" The séance ended, but as it did, a violent thunderstorm erupted, drenching the rooftop gathering and filling the sky with thunder and lightning. Strangely, the storm did not appear anywhere else in Hollywood—only directly above the Knickerbocker Hotel. Houdini Séances continue to this day.

✠

In 1975, vandals smashed the marble bust on Houdini's grave and it lay in disrepair until it was finally repaired, thanks to a donation of $10,000 from a fan, the magician David Copperfield.

POPE JOHN PAUL II

John Paul II had been ill for almost a decade. In February 2005, however, his health took a definite turn for the worst. Once an athlete and always a strong speaker, he was now racked with arthritis and Parkinson's disease. Twice in that month he had been rushed to Rome's Gemelli Hospital with breathing problems and had to have a tracheotomy. The operation seemed to drain his strength and on two occasions, he failed to address crowds in St. Peter's Square.

By Thursday, March 31, journalists were being told that the pope was "sick, very sick." On Wednesday he had made a distressing appearance at the window of the Vatican, trying to speak, but emitting only a muffled sound. Doctors had inserted a feeding tube into his stomach to try to boost his energy levels, but he then developed a urinary infection and high fever that soon precipitated heart failure and kidney problems.

His condition was now regarded as "very serious." He had received the last rites at 5:17 P.M. on that Thursday evening and, according to Father Konrad Hejmo, a leader of the Polish community in Rome, he was "ready to die." He added that the pontiff was "fully conscious, lucid and extremely serene." The pope had rejected another visit to the hospital, choosing to die in the apartments he had lived in for the 26 years of his pontificate. As Navarro-Valls announced the pope's condition to be "serious, but stable," up to ten thousand people gathered in St. Peter's

Square, gazing up at the windows of the pope's apartments in the Vatican. A fresh update some time later reported that he remained conscious, had celebrated Mass, and had asked for the Fourteen Stations of the Cross to be read to him. Navarro-Valls announced that he also asked that the scripture of the so-called "Third Hour" be read to him, a passage significant because, according to tradition, Christ died at three o'clock in the afternoon. "This is surely an image I have never seen in these 26 years," the usually unflappable Navarro-Valls said. Breaking down, he had to leave the press conference.

At around five o'clock on Friday evening the Pope's condition worsened; his blood pressure was lower and his breathing had by now become shallow. At a special mass in a Rome cathedral, Cardinal Camillo Ruini said that John Paul II was already "seeing and touching the Lord," and up to seventy thousand people gathered outside the Vatican for an all-night vigil. At times this huge crowd was so silent that the water could be heard trickling down from the fountains in the square. At other times, the crowd sang "Stay with us!"

Vatican officials denied reports in the media that John Paul was already dead, but speaking to the crowd, Archbishop Angelo Comastri said, "This evening, or tonight, Christ is opening the door to the Pope."

The world prayed for him. In Wadowice, Poland, people left school and work early and went to church to pray for their native son. In the Philippines, special masses were celebrated. At the Church of the Assumption in Lagos, sub-Saharan Africa's most populous city of over 13 million, about two hundred Nigerians in Western clothes and bright traditional African robes sat on wooden benches, offering prayers for the pope at a midday Mass. The White House said President Bush and his wife were praying for him and that the world's concern was "a testimony to his greatness." Even China, which bars its Catholics from recognizing the authority of the Vatican, expressed concern for the pope's condition.

On the morning of Saturday, April 2, Cardinal Joseph Ratzinger visited the pope and reported that "he knows he is dying" and has "said his last good-bye." The world watched and waited.

In his last hours, the pontiff lay in bed amid a tangle of medical tubes and probes. His long-serving private secretary, Archbishop Dziwisz, did not leave his side and held his hand, while around them, tearful Polish nuns recited the rosary. He was drifting in and out of consciousness, but, it was firmly stated, he was not in a coma. His general heart and breathing conditions were by now very serious. At eight o'clock he was once again given the Sacrament for the Sick and Dying— the last rites—and listened as his favorite passages from the Scriptures were read.

Shortly after 9:30 on the night of Saturday, April 2, John Paul grasped Archbishop Dziwisz's hand, stared at the window of his sparsely furnished bedroom, in the direction of the crowd gathered in St. Peter's Square below. As the crowd finished reciting the rosary below, he raised his hand to offer a blessing, whispered, "Amen," and died. It was 9:37 P.M.

THE FUNERAL

Rome and large parts of the world came to a stop for the funeral of John Paul II on a blustery Friday, April 9. Four kings, five queens, one heir to the throne (the Prince of Wales), and seventy presidents and prime ministers attended. St. Peter's and its environs were filled with some three hundred and fifty thousand people, mostly young and Slavic, who waved flags and chanted the late pope's name. "*Santo, subito!*" ("Sainthood now!") was on their lips. In Kraków, eight hundred thousand people watched the funeral on giant screens. John Paul's lead-lined coffin was made of cypress wood with a simple cross and the letter M—for "Mary"—carved into it.

POST MORTEM

The news of John Paul II's death was immediately announced to the seventy thousand people gathered in St. Peter's Square and was met with long applause, an Italian sign of respect. Bells tolled and many people wept openly. "Our Holy Father, John Paul, has returned to the house of the Father," Archbishop Leonardo Sandri told the crowds.

✠

There is a strict ritual after the death of a pope. A pronouncement is made in Latin that the pope is dead, and it is certified by a physician. The Camerlengo, or chamberlain, the most important Vatican official until a new pope is elected, then calls out the pontiff's baptismal name—Karol for Pope John Paul II—three times to confirm there is no response. In the past, the

Camerlengo struck a silver hammer against the pope's forehead to confirm his death, but it's unclear if the ritual is still active.

The Camerlengo then destroys the symbols of that papacy: the Pescatorio, or Ring of the Fisherman, and the dies used to make lead seals for apostolic letters. The pope's quarters are sealed and funeral arrangements are begun by the Camerlengo. Vatican flags fly at half-staff and, according to tradition, the bronze door at St. Peter's Basilica is closed. An official nine-day mourning period, known as the *novemediales*, follows the death of a pope, a tradition dating back to ancient Rome and a ceremony held nine days after death. The pope's body lies in state in St. Peter's Basilica in the Clementine Chapel, which was begun by Michelangelo and completed by Giacomo Della Porta for the Jubilee in 1600. The funeral and burial must be held between the fourth and sixth day after death, according to rules established in 1996, and most popes in recent centuries have chosen to be buried beneath St. Peter's Basilica. After the funeral in St. Peter's Square, the lead-lined coffin is carried through the "door of death" on the left side of the main altar in the Basilica. As a single bell is tolled, the coffin is lowered into a marble sarcophagus and covered by a huge stone slab.

On April 19, the second day of the Conclave of Cardinals, the hard-line German Cardinal, Joseph Ratzinger, was elected pope Benedict XVI on the fourth ballot. It was one of the briefest conclaves of modern times.

After the global fame his desert exploits had brought him, T.E. Lawrence's descent in ranks bemused people. To George Bernard Shaw, it was as if Nelson, after the Battle of the Nile, had insisted on being put at the tiller of a canal barge; according to him, it was "a maddening masquerade." But Lawrence simply loved being in the Royal Air France. He told one journalist, "I'm in the R.A.F. because I like it and when people offer me larger boots and talk of my wasting my 'talents' in the ranks, I comfort myself with the sure knowledge that there's nothing else my talented self wants to do."

Therefore, it was with no little distress that he arrived at the end of his R.A.F. career—"the only really contented years of my life," as he described them. He had been moved about the country in the last few years and now, in 1935, he was back at Clouds Hill, the cottage he had purchased for himself about a mile from Bovington Camp in Dorset, and was forced to ease himself into frugal retirement. At Clouds Hill, he received visitors from the artistic and literary world. Here, too, he engaged another private, John Bruce, to severely birch him every day, a ritual his brother ascribed to the methods used by saints to purge themselves of the urge for sex.

Some tried to get him back into public life. In one of the last letters he received, his close friend Lady Astor wrote to him: "If you come to Cliveden the last Saturday in May, you will never regret it." Listing the people who would be there—among them Stanley Baldwin, who had been prime minister and was about to be again—she suggested that the government would be keen for him to take part in the reorganization of the armed forces. Characteristically, Lawrence replied, "No: wild mares would not at present take me away from Clouds Hill. It is an earthly paradise and I am staying here until I feel qualified for it. Also there is something broken in the works, as I told you: my will, I think. In this mood I would not take on any job at all. So do not commit yourself to advocating me, lest I prove a nonstarter."

Henry Williamson, author of *Tarka the Otter* and a close friend of Lawrence, was a supporter of Oswald Mosley's British fascist movement and had displayed some sympathy for Adolf Hitler. He had been deeply moved by his experiences on the western front in the First World War and feared that another war between Britain and Germany would bring the end of civilization and the unstoppable rise of Bolshevism. He wrote to Lawrence at the beginning of May, asking whether he would be interested in meeting Hitler, believing that Hitler could be influenced by a man like Lawrence. Lawrence answered by telegram, inviting Williamson to lunch at Clouds Hill. It was the last correspondence he wrote.

Pat Knowles lived across the road from Clouds Hill and was a friend and aide to Lawrence. He described the morning of Tuesday, May 13 as Lawrence set out to post his telegram to Williamson: "He came across to me shortly before he went and asked if there was anything I wanted and shortly afterwards I heard him move off. Well, it was one of those bright, clear days in May when the wind was southerly and it was very pleasant, and I could hear the drill sergeants on the squares. And later I heard the motorcycle coming back. I heard the engine suddenly race and then stop."

On the road from Bovington Camp, Lawrence had swerved to avoid two errand boys. He clipped the wheel of one of their bikes and lost control of his Brough (the seventh Brough he had owned in the past 12 years, all called by the biblical name "Boanerges"—"the sons of thunder"). He flew over the handlebars of the motorbike and hit the ground hard, knocking himself unconscious.

Lawrence lay in a coma for six days at Bovington Camp Hospital before dying shortly after eight o'clock on the morning of Sunday, May 19. He was 46 years old.

THE FUNERAL

Lawrence was buried at Moreton Church, near Clouds Hill, on May 21, 1935. He had expressly requested that there be no wreaths or flowers.

His pallbearers were British diplomat Sir Ronald Storrs; artist Eric Kennington; Colonel Stewart F. Newcombe, aircraftman Bradbury; Arthur Russell of the Tank Corps; and Pat Knowles.

Among the mourners were Winston Churchill, Lady Astor, and the artist Augustus John. The only biographical detail in the inscription on the headstone states that he had been a fellow of All Souls College in Oxford.

BRANDON LEE

In March 1993, filming of *The Crow*, starring 28-year-old Brandon Lee, was nearing completion at Carolco Studios in Wilmington, North Carolina. It had been a troublesome shoot, accidents plaguing the set before and after shooting. On February 1, the first day of shooting, a carpenter had received serious burns when a scissor lift he was driving hit some high-voltage power lines. On March 13, severe storms had destroyed a number of the elaborate sets. Other mishaps included a disgruntled carpenter driving his car into the studio's plaster shop, one worker accidentally stabbing his hand with a screwdriver, and a stuntman breaking several ribs after plunging through a roof.

Eight days before completion of the film, Brandon Lee, son of the late martial arts movie phenomenon Bruce Lee, was due to film a scene that involved a close-up scene of a gun being fired. Dummy cartridges were to be used in the scene. These are perfect for close-up shots because they contain the actual projectile but no gunpowder. Therefore, it looks as if there are real bullets in the chamber.

On the day in question, however, the studio's props department had run out of dummy cartridges. To save time and money —the production would have to be shut down for the night if they had to wait for the cartridges to be delivered—it was decided to remove the gunpowder from live rounds and replace the bullet tips.

The close-up scenes were completed and the dummy bullets were replaced with blanks loaded with highly explosive powder that would create the smoke and flash that a real gun would give. This was what was needed for the next scene which called for a wide shot of Lee's character being shot. He was required to enter a room where actor Michael Massee was to shoot him. Fatally, no one from the inexperienced crew thought to check the gun's barrel.

Lee, dressed in a black leather jacket, boots, and a T-shirt bearing the phrase "Hangman's Joke," entered the room carrying a bag of groceries. Massee fired the gun at him from a distance of about fifteen feet and Lee set off the "squib," a device to simulate bullets hitting the bag he was carrying. Tragically, when the dummies were put in the revolver, a piece of one of the bullets that had been tampered with by the props department had broken off and become lodged in the barrel or cylinder.

Lee collapsed, blood pouring from his right side. He groaned and signaled with his arm that he had been hit, but no one noticed. It was only when the director shouted "Cut!" and the actor failed to rise that they knew there was a problem.

An ambulance rushed Lee to the nearby New Hanover Regional Medical Center. He was still alive despite the large wound in his right abdomen and serious damage to his stomach and vital organs. The bullet had finally come to rest next to his spine and emergency surgery was performed to stop the severe internal hemorrhaging. But efforts were futile and he died in the hospital at three minutes past one on the afternoon of March 31, 1993, a little more than 12 hours after the shooting.

THE FUNERAL

Brandon Lee's body was flown back to Washington State where he was buried on April 3 next to his father, Bruce Lee, in Lake View Cemetery. The next day a memorial service was held at the house of his actor friend, Polly Bergen, in the Hollywood Hills. Among those attending were David Carradine, Kiefer Sutherland, David Hasselhoff, Lou Diamond Phillips, and Steven Seagal.

POST MORTEM

The subsequent investigation failed to conclusively determine how the bullet tip had become dislodged. The blank cartridge had enough force when fired to propel the bullet tip into the young actor's body.

Investigators concluded that it was an accidental death caused by negligence on the part of the film crew.

Linda Lee Caldwell, Brandon Lee's mother, filed a civil suit against the studio, but it was settled out of court.

Both Lee's mother and his fiancée, Eliza Hutton, were supportive of the completion of the film. This required some rewrites, shooting remaining scenes with a double, and digitally adding Lee's face into a few key scenes. Paramount Pictures was concerned about marketing the film and after several other studios declined, Miramax, renowned for selling difficult, small independent films, took it on. They did not use Lee's death in any way and the only mention is in the closing credits where there is a dedication "For Brandon and Eliza." *The Crow* was eventually released on May 11, 1994. Unsurprisingly, it did well at the box office, with final takings of over fifty million.

✠

Some say that the scene where Brandon Lee was killed is still in the final film. However, this is unlikely to be true and it is believed that the segment was destroyed.

THE CONSPIRACY THEORY

Brandon Lee believed his family was jinxed by a curse made against his grandfather when he angered some Chinese businessmen.

Some people claim that Lee was murdered by the same Chinese mafia that are said to have caused the death of his father in 1973 as punishment for his exposure of ancient martial arts secrets on film.

Others say that Brandon Lee was murdered by gangsters with ties to the Hong Kong movie industry, who had been angered by his refusal to work in their films.

BRUCE LEE

I n May 1973, during the final dubbing of Bruce Lee's film
Enter the Dragon, the actor suffered a sudden attack of seizures and a cerebral edema. Fortunately, the attack was not
fatal, but the neurosurgeon who saved his life, Dr. Peter Wu,
said that he removed a considerable amount of hashish from
Lee's stomach. The actor had been chewing hashish to calm
himself in the face of escalating international celebrity.

On July 20, 1973, Lee was busying himself with ideas for
his next film, *Game of Death*. At two in the afternoon, he held a
meeting at home with film producer Raymond Chow. The two
men worked until four and then they drove to the apartment
of Betty Ting Pei, a Taiwanese actress who was to be one of the
stars of the film. The three worked on the script before Chow
had to leave for a meeting, agreeing to meet the two for dinner
later with former James Bond star George Lazenby, with whom
Lee was planning to make a film.

Lee had been complaining of a headache and Ting Pei gave
him a pill containing Equagesic, a kind of super aspirin. He had
consumed nothing other than a couple of soft drinks.

At around 7:30, he lay down to have a nap and was still asleep
when Chow called to ask why the pair had not turned up for
dinner as arranged. Ting Pei told Chow that she had tried to
wake Lee, but had been unable to do so. Chow hurried over to
the apartment and, also failing to wake the actor, immediately

summoned medical help. After trying to revive Lee for ten minutes an ambulance was called to take him to Queen Elizabeth Hospital. He was dead on arrival, just 32 years old.

THE FUNERAL

Thousands lined the streets in Hong Kong to honor his symbolic burial parade, and scores of spectators were injured in the crush. Steel barriers were erected along the coffin's route to restrain the crowd.

Pallbearers at Lee's funeral in Seattle in July 1973 included Steve McQueen, James Coburn, Chuck Norris and George Lazenby. He was laid to rest in Lake View Cemetery, wearing the traditional Chinese outfit he wore in *Enter The Dragon*.

POST MORTEM

Bruce Lee died of a brain aneurysm in the vicinity of the cerebral edema that had first surfaced in May 1973. Whether it was present from birth or caused later by a blow to the head is pure conjecture. In any case, with a damaged blood vessel in his head capable of exploding at any moment, he had been living on borrowed time.

✠

Foul play was immediately suspected. Raymond Chow appeared on television to try to settle the public furor that quickly developed. He explained what happened, omitting only the fact that Lee had not died at home. The press soon uncovered the truth, however, and demanded to know what Chow was trying to cover up, sensing that the actor had been having an affair with Ting Pei.

✠

Medical authorities came up with five reasons for Bruce Lee's death. They all agreed that it was caused by a cerebral edema —a swelling of the brain caused by a congestion of fluid. But what caused the edema was not so certain. The ensuing autopsy found traces of cannabis in Lee's stomach, but the significance of this discovery is debatable. Some believe the cannabis caused a chemical reaction that led to the cerebral edema, but the coroner's inquiry refutes this theory. In fact, one doctor was quoted as saying that the cannabis in Lee's stomach was "no more significant than if Bruce had drunk a cup of tea that day."

✠

Dr. R.R. Lycette of Queen Elizabeth Hospital concluded that Lee's death resulted from a hypersensitivity to one or more of the compounds found in the headache tablet he had consumed that afternoon. Although his skull showed no injury, his brain had swollen considerably, from 1,400 to 1,575 grams. None of the blood vessels were blocked or broken, so the possibility of a hemorrhage was ruled out. All of his internal organs were meticulously examined, and the only "foreign" substance to be found was the Equagesic. He thinks Bruce was very vulnerable to the effects of drugs due to his extremely low body fat. Dr. Donald Langford, Lee's physician in Hong Kong, said that Bruce's body had less than one percent body fat, that "it was obscene how little body fat he had." Bruce Lee weighed only around 128 pounds at the time of his death.

✠

R.D. Teare, a professor of forensic medicine at the University of London who had overseen more than ninety-thousand autopsies, was called in and declared that it was impossible for cannabis to be a factor in Lee's death. In Teare's opinion, the edema was caused by hypersensitivity to either meprobamate or aspirin, or a combination of both. His view was accepted by authorities, and a verdict of "misadventure" was given.

THE CONSPIRACY THEORY

When Bruce Lee died speculation was rife that he had been killed by:

* Hong Kong triads because he refused to pay them the protection money that Chinese film stars were expected to pay.
* An angry martial artist's *dim mak* or death touch strike in a challenge match because he had given up the secrets of the martial arts community by teaching foreigners.
* *Oni*—Japanese demons or evil spirits.
* The curse of a haunted house that he had just bought in Hong Kong.

The health of Vladimir Ilich Lenin, chairman of the Council of People's Commissars—leader of the Union of Soviet Socialist Republics—had never been great, but by mid-1921 it was in drastic decline. He was suffering from severe headaches and insomnia and had been the victim of a series of small heart attacks. Distressingly for a workaholic like him, it was becoming increasingly difficult to do a full day's work. In the past, he would force sick members of his government to go to sanatoria or hospitals and when he told the Politburo about his problems, he was instructed to take time off.

He did so, but managed to set up a regime which allowed him to carry on working for a time, if not at full stretch, in the place known as the "Big House" in Gorki. As time went on, however, for the first time in his life, he began to lose the will to work and his doctors seemed unable to diagnose what was wrong with him. He endured frequent episodes of obsessiveness and wondered whether he was, in fact, going mad. But above all Lenin feared a lingering paralyzed death. To allay his fears, he solicited a promise from his comrade Stalin to give him poison should he request it.

He returned to the Kremlin where the diagnoses were whittled down eventually to just a few—syphilis; neurasthenia or nervous exhaustion; residual damage from an operation he had had to remove a bullet from his neck; and cerebral arteriosclerosis, the illness that had killed his father.

On March 5, 1923, his condition worsened, and by March 7 he was beginning to lose the use of the extremities on the right side of his body. Soon he was unable to speak and had to be carried everywhere. On March 10, a huge spasm took away all movement from his right side and he could only move his left hand with difficulty. Worse, he was suffering from unbearable headaches.

On May 15, 1923, he was moved once again from the Kremlin to the Big House and, apart from several excursions—one to the Kremlin for the last time—that was where he remained.

By January 21, 1924, there was cause for hope. Lenin had not had a collapse for a month and had even been getting about with the help of a stick. However, waking at 10:30 A.M. that morning, he complained of feeling unwell while drinking some black coffee. He went back to bed and slept until three o'clock. Feeling better when he woke, he drank a little more coffee and had some clear soup. His physician, Dr. Osipov, found nothing to worry about when he went to Lenin's room to carry out his daily examination. His pulse was a little fast, but that was all.

Then, around 5.40 P.M. Lenin, propped up in bed, felt the onset of an attack. The three doctors on duty—Osipov, Förster, Yelistratov, and their assistant Vladimir Rukavishnikov—held a hasty consultation, but there was little they could do as Lenin fell into a coma. It was not the first time this had happened, but this time he remained comatose much longer than before. When his heartbeat was found to be slowing down, Maria Ilinichna, his younger sister, sent out for camphor to help restore it.

Fellow Politburo member Nikolai Bukharin was staying at the Big House to do some writing and, hearing that something was happening, ran across to investigate. By this time, Lenin's temperature had risen sharply and, covered in sweat, he tossed and turned in his narrow bed, roaring in pain. Bukharin wrote: "When I ran into Ilich's room, full of doctors and stacked with medicines, Ilich let out a last sigh. His face fell back and went terribly white. He let out a wheeze, his hands dropped. Ilich, Ilich was no more."

The doctors lifted his eyelids, looking for signs of life, but Vladimir Ilich Ulyanov Lenin's struggle was finally over. It was 6:50 P.M.

The Funeral

On January 23, 1924, Lenin's coffin was taken by train to Moscow. His corpse was laid out in the House of Trade Unions and mourners flooded into the capital from all over the U.S.S.R.

The funeral took place on January 27, the coldest day of the year—so cold that trumpeters had to smear vodka on their mouthpieces to prevent them from freezing to their lips.

Among the pallbearers were Grigory Zinoviev, Stalin, Bukharin, and Vyacheslav Molotov. The entire country came to a standstill. Trains stopped in their tracks and factory whistles and hooters sounded in all the towns and villages. At four o'clock on the dark afternoon, Lenin was lowered into the earth in a vault that had been prepared in front of the Kremlin in Red Square.

Post Mortem

On the orders of the Politburo, Lenin's body was dug up and
kept on ice in the Central Moscow mortuary until scientists
had worked out how to embalm it so that it could be put
on permanent display in a mausoleum in Red Square. The
Bolshevik leadership claimed it was only responding to requests
by factory workers, but in reality, it was Stalin's idea. He
thought that it would serve as a unifying presence for citizens
of the Soviet Union as well as Communists around the world.
Petrograd, formerly St. Petersburg, was renamed
Leningrad in his honor.

An Institute of the Brain was established in his honor and
thirty thousand slices of his brain tissue were collected so that
research might be carried out into the secrets of his genius.

The Mausoleum Group, responsible for looking after
Lenin's body, also mummified and helps to maintain the bodies
of Mao Tse-tung and Ho Chi Minh. Some say that they keep
Lenin look-a-likes in the basement of his tomb
in case his body crumbles. This is denied.

LIBERACE

He was born Wladziu Valentino Liberace, but when he was not being called "Mr. Showmanship" or "the Candelabra Kid" or "Mr Box Office" or "the Guru of Glitter," or—close friends only—"Lee," he was known by just one name—Liberace.

He had been a child prodigy, playing piano by ear at the age of four, and at the age of twenty he made his solo debut with the Chicago Symphony Orchestra. Soon, his signature candelabra glittering on his grand piano, he was tickling the ivories in his semi-classical fashion in clubs and hotels across America. By 1950, his name changed to simply Liberace, he had added an element of comedy and some singing to his act, as well as flamboyant clothes, and began to be a regular on the new medium of television. *The Dinah Shore Show* was America's biggest show at the time and Liberace's appearances between 1952 and 1956 made him a huge star. In 1955 he became the highest-paid performer in Las Vegas, earning $50,000 a week. By the 1960's, he was America's highest-paid entertainer, earning five million dollars a year.

In a time when disclosure of homosexuality was guaranteed to bring down the final curtain on a performer's career, Liberace's sexual tendencies were a subject of great speculation. Nonetheless, he resolutely denied being gay, to the extent of taking British tabloid *The Daily Mirror* to court when it hinted he might just conceivably not be completely heterosexual. Columnist Cassandra described the entertainer as a "deadly, winking, sniggering, snuggling, chromium-plated, scent-impregnated, luminous, quivering, giggling, fruit-flavored, mincing, ice-covered heap of mother love, a sugary mountain of jingling claptrap wrapped in such a preposterous clown." Liberace denied everything and won.

In 1982 his closet door swung wide open when his former lover of five years, Scott Thorson, whose face Liberace's plastic surgeon had remodeled to make him look like the pianist, sued for palimony of $113,000,000. Liberace denied Thorson's accusations before settling out of court for $95,000. No slouch in sleaze, Thorson would later claim to have had a relationship with Michael Jackson and was a key prosecution witness in the notorious Wonderland quadruple murder case involving a lot of drugs and the porn legend John Holmes.

By 1980 Liberace had found another love—18 year-old Cary James. However, in 1985 the couple tested HIV-positive. Liberace was ill and had lost fifty pounds. His condition was not helped by the shock of the death of his old friend Rock Hudson, the actor and fellow closet homosexual, with whom he is reputed to have had a relationship. Still, as he rehearsed for his last-ever concert at Radio City Music Hall, he refused to admit that he was gay. To close friends, Liberace said, "I don't want to be remembered as an old queen who died of AIDS." To the outside world, his management attributed the weight loss to the "watermelon diet" that was all the rage in Hollywood at the time.

When Liberace's sister Angelina realized in January 1987 that her brother was very ill indeed, she insisted on him being taken to the Eisenhower Medical Center in Rancho Mirage, California. He was immediately quarantined, confirming to the expectant members of the press that the pianist was suffering from AIDS. Three days later, he returned to his lavishly appointed house at 226 West Alejo Road in Palm Springs where the media swarmed and almost a hundred of his most ardent fans waited for news. He had come home to die.

Reportedly, he saw out his last hours watching reruns of his favorite television show, *The Golden Girls*, in the company of his sister Angela; his sister-in-law Dora, widow of his beloved brother, George; a man called Jamie Wyatt, described as his "friend and long-time companion," and his 27 dogs.

He died at 2:05 P.M. on February 4, 1987. He was 67 years old.

THE FUNERAL

Liberace was buried on February 7 in Forest Lawn Cemetery in Hollywood Hills in Los Angeles. Robert Goulet delivered a eulogy and the pianist was buried wearing his wig, a white tuxedo, and full stage makeup. Photos of his last boyfriend and Wrinkles, his favorite of all his dogs, were placed in the casket with him. His extravagant tombstone is made of white marble and a classical statue stands on top of it. It is decorated with his signature, complete with scribbled grand piano and his trademark candelabra. His brother George and his mother lie beside him.

Post Mortem

Liberace's doctors listed his cause of death as "cardiac arrest due to cardiac failure, due to sub-acute encephalopathy with a contributing condition of aplastic anemia." His body was swiftly removed to the Forest Lawn Cemetery in Los Angeles County for burial, but knowing that the entertainer was suffering from AIDS, the coroner in Riverside County insisted on the body being brought back for an autopsy. Coroner Raymond Carillo stated subsequently at a news conference that Liberace had actually died of "cytomegalovirus pneumonia due to human immunodeficiency virus disease, an opportunistic disease caused by acquired immune deficiency syndrome."

He continued: "Cytomegalovirus is a common virus that affects more than half the adult population without ill effects. However, it can be fatal to people whose immune system is weakened by the AIDS virus." He accused Liberace's doctors of covering up the real cause of death.

✠

Other ailments contributing to Liberace's death included lung and heart disease and a hardening of a valve in his heart.

A pril 14, 1865, was a beautiful spring day. As usual, Abraham Lincoln, the 16th president of the United States, rose at seven. He was feeling good as he sat down at his mahogany desk to deal with some work before breakfast. A few days previously, General Ulysses Grant had accepted the surrender of Robert E. Lee, commander in chief of the Confederate armies, and Lincoln was now awaiting news that another southern general, Joseph E. Johnston, had also capitulated in North Carolina.

Lincoln gave instructions for Assistant Secretary of State Frederick Seward to call a cabinet meeting for eleven o'clock that morning and wrote a message inviting General Grant to attend. At eight, Lincoln had breakfast—always one egg and one cup of coffee—with his wife, Mary, and his sons, Robert and Tad, before returning to work in his office.

The papers that morning announced that the president, along with General Grant and his wife, would be attending the comedy *Our American Cousin* at Ford's Theater that evening, and Lincoln sent a messenger to the theater to reserve the State Box for him and his party.

At the end of the cabinet meeting, around two o'clock, Grant informed Lincoln that he and his wife had decided to visit their children and were no longer able to go to the theater. Secretary of War Stanton, overhearing plans for the theater visit, pleaded with the president not to endanger himself by going out at night—these were unstable times. Lincoln himself became reluctant to attend, as he told his wife over lunch, but he changed his mind and invited Major Henry Rathbone and his fiancée, Clara Harris, to join them.

Finishing work around four in the afternoon, he and Mary enjoyed a carriage ride, but after dinner Mary complained of a headache and again considered not going to the theater. Lincoln demurred, complaining that he was a little tired, but then said he needed cheering up and would go without her. Mary again changed her mind and decided she would accompany him after all.

Still anxious for news from North Carolina Lincoln, accompanied by his bodyguard William Crook, made his way to the War Department, but nothing had been heard. On their return journey, Crook joined the voices fearful for the president's safety, begging him to cancel the theater visit. When Lincoln rejected his pleas, Crook asked if he could go along as extra security. Again, Lincoln refused his request, believing that with a guard posted outside the State Box in the theater he would be safe.

It was shortly after eight when the Lincolns left for the theater. Mary was wearing a black-and-white striped silk dress and a matching bonnet, and Lincoln wore white kid gloves and a black overcoat made of wool, tailored for him by Brooks Brothers of New York. They took their seats after the play had started but the performance stopped as the orchestra burst into a rendition of "Hail to the Chief." The door to the box was then closed but, crucially, not locked. Moreover, unluckily for Lincoln, the police guard that night was a man reputed to be fond of drink and, true to form, at the intermissions, John Parker abandoned his post in the hallway that led to the president's box and walked across the road to the Taltavul's Star Saloon. When the curtains rose on the play's third act, he was not at his post.

Mary sat very close to her husband, holding his hand. She whispered to him, "What will Miss Harris think of my hanging on to you so?" He replied, "She won't think anything about it." It was about 10:15 and onstage, actor Harry Hawk was saying, "Don't know the manners of good society, eh? Well, I guess I know enough to turn you inside out, old gal—you sockdologizing old mantrap!"

At this point the door to the box burst open and Lincoln's assassin, the ex-actor John Wilkes Booth, stepped in, pointed a derringer at the back of the president's head and pulled the trigger. As Mary screamed and reached out to her husband he slumped forward in his seat, and the man pulled out a dagger, yelling: "*Sic semper tyrannis!*" ("Thus always to tyrants!") He slashed Rathbone's arm to the bone and then leapt from the box, catching his spur on a flag and breaking his left shin as he crashed to the stage. He managed to escape through the rear stage door.

The unconscious Lincoln had been shot behind the left ear, the bullet tearing through that side of his brain. He was carried across the street to the Petersen House and into the room of a War Department clerk where, breathing heavily, he had to be laid on the bed diagonally as he was too tall for it.

Six surgeons were present, one of whom, Dr. Hall, announced that to all intents and purposes the president was already dead, but that he might live another three hours or so. He had been stripped of his clothes and his face was calm, although after a while, his right eye began to swell and his face became discolored.

The speaker of the Senate and other members of the Cabinet arrived and a guard was posted at the door, as there was a large, excitable crowd gathering outside. This room, like every other room in the house, was by now full to overflowing.

Every hour, Mrs. Lincoln would return to her husband's bed-side. At around seven in the morning, Mary visited his bedside for the last time. Lincoln's son Robert stood at the head of the bed, sobbing.

At 7:22 A.M. on the morning of April 15, 1865, President Abraham Lincoln expired, lying diagonally on a strange bed that was much too small for his giant frame.

THE FUNERAL

Lincoln's funeral train left Washington on April 21, 1865, to retrace the 1,654-mile route he had traveled as president-elect in 1861. The *Lincoln Special*, whose engine had Lincoln's photograph over the cowcatcher, carried approximately three hundred mourners. His son Willie's coffin was also on board. Willie, who had died in the White House in 1862 at the age of 11, had been disinterred and was to be buried with his father in Springfield. A Guard of Honor accompanied the remains. Robert Lincoln rode on the train to Baltimore but then returned to Washington.

In Baltimore, approximately ten thousand people viewed the coffin in three hours. Forty thousand people lined the streets of Harrisburg as it passed. In Philadelphia it was estimated that three-hundred thousand people filed past the coffin and in New York the number was five-hundred thousand. Hundreds of thousands of people viewed it as it was borne across the Union before finally being laid to rest in Springfield.

Post Mortem

After exiting Ford's Theater, John Wilkes Booth mounted a horse that was being held by an innocent theater employee and escaped to the south. On April 26, he was shot dead by Boston Corbett of the 16th New York Cavalry unit near Bowling Green, Virginia.

✛

Eight conspirators were tried for Lincoln's assassination. All were found guilty and four were hanged, including Mary Surratt, the first woman executed by the U.S. government.

✛

A few days before his death, Lincoln told his wife of a dream he had in which he saw a funeral in the White House. "Who is dead?" he asked of a soldier. "The president, killed by an assassin!" was the soldier's reply.

✛

Edwin Booth, John Wilkes Booth's brother, died on June 7, 1893. Two days later, at the very moment Edwin's casket was being carried from the Little Church Around the Corner in New York City, all three floors of Ford's Theater collapsed, killing 22 people and injuring 68 others.

The young couple (Henry Rathbone and Clara Harris) who attended *Our American Cousin* with the Lincolns were married two years after the assassination and had three children. Rathbone suffered from severe mood swings and was probably taking an opiate that could be purchased over the counter in the nineteenth century. In 1882 he was appointed to the post of U.S. Consul General to Germany, but on December 23, 1883, he went berserk, tried to kill his children, then shot and stabbed his wife to death, before finally stabbing himself. He spent the rest of his life in an asylum for the criminally insane.

In May 1875, an insanity trial for Mary Todd Lincoln, the president's wife, was held in Chicago. The jury found Mrs. Lincoln "insane and a fit person to be in a state hospital for the insane." Mary spent the next several months in an asylum in Batavia, Illinois.

William A. Petersen, the German tailor in whose house the president died, committed suicide. His body, filled with laudanum (a mixture of alcohol and opium derivatives), was found on the grounds of the Smithsonian Institution on June 18, 1871.

✠

Robert Lincoln, the president's son, was in the White House when his father was shot. On July 2, 1881, Robert was with President James A. Garfield at Washington's Baltimore and Potomac Railroad Station when the president was shot by the assassin Charles J. Guiteau. Finally, on September 6,

1901, when President William McKinley was shot by Leon F. Czolgosz at the Pan American Exposition in Buffalo, Robert was on a train just arriving in Buffalo.

Several American towns apparently heard reports of Lincoln's assassination before it actually happened. For example, George Kulzer, a pioneer of Stearns County, Minnesota, told the following story about the town of St. Joseph in Minnesota: "Early in the morning on Wednesday, the 14th, people were horror-stricken to hear that President Lincoln had been assassinated. No one knew how the news had arrived, since we had no telegraph. Later we heard that Mr. Lincoln had indeed been assassinated, but not until late in the evening of that day."

Marie Antoinette just did not get it. As the French Revolution raged around her, she was completely unable to comprehend the impact it was having on France, and although it is unlikely that she uttered the famous words often attributed to her—"Let them eat cake!"—when people marched in protest at the price of bread—there can be little doubt she would have sympathized with the sentiment.

She was criticized for her extravagant and unconventional lifestyle and was disliked for her opposition to measures designed to ease France's economic difficulties. When things finally began to turn nasty, she and her husband, Louis XVI, tried to flee the country but were caught and arrested. Louis was subsequently tried and executed and Marie Antoinette was imprisoned.

On October 12, 1793, Marie Antoinette underwent a secret preliminary interrogation in the Conciergerie, a prison on the Quai d'Horloge. Once the property of the person in charge of the king of France's residence, since the late 14 century it had been a dank, gothic prison. She was taken from her bed and led before the young president of the Revolutionary Tribunal, Martial Joseph Armand Herman, an ally of the dreaded Robespierre. The usual accusations were leveled at her and, as ever, she denied all of the charges.

The Conciergerie was little more than an antechamber to

the Revolutionary Tribunal that took place in the prison's great chamber. On Monday, October 14, she was led through the prison and into the crowded courtroom where her appearance caused a sensation. Contrary to what the spectators had anticipated, the queen looked haggard—her features were sunken and her hair was white. She was clad in a worn, patched black dress and swore the oath in the name of Marie Antoinette of Lorraine and Austria, widow of the King of France, born in Vienna. She said she was "about 38" and, according to the hostile newspaper *L'Anti-Fédéraliste*, she glanced around the courtroom with "the serenity that habitual crime gives." Her armchair was positioned on a platform, so that she was visible to all, although the market women in the great chamber complained that she should be made to stand so that they could get a better look.

Marie Antoinette answered every question with the words "I do not believe so" or "I don't remember." But, most of what was attested to by the forty witnesses who were called was not much more than gossip. Among other things, she was accused of attending orgies, organizing feasts, passing money to the Austrian emperor, and getting the Swiss Guards drunk so that they would massacre French people. Most outrageous of all, however, were the accusations that she had an incestuous relationship with her young son, Louis Charles. Proceedings continued until 11 P.M., with little in the way of evidence being divulged.

The next morning, Marie Antoinette was back in court before she had even had a chance to eat breakfast. She spent the day again denying all charges and refuting all of the slurs on her character and by midnight, she had been in court for 16 hours.

After the cross-examination of the fortieth witness, she was asked if she had anything to say. She told the court that she was guilty of nothing more than being the king's wife.

Marie Antoinette was not present for the summing-up to the jurors by Herman. She was convinced that nothing had really been proved against her and that she would merely be sent into exile. But, on returning to the courtroom, she was shocked to find that she had been found guilty on all counts. The prosecutor asked for the death penalty and it was readily granted. The queen simply shook her head when she was asked if she had anything to say. At four in the morning on October 16, she walked out of the courtroom, past the barriers that held back the people, doing her best to keep her head held high.

Back in her cell she was given writing materials previously denied to her and wrote a last letter to Madame Elisabeth, her sister-in-law. In it she tells her how calm she felt and how clear her conscience was, regretting only that she was leaving her children. She left a message for her son, Louis Charles—"Let my son never forget his father's last words: never try to avenge our deaths."

Rosalie Lamorlière, her servant, came to her cell at 7 A.M. The Queen refused food at first, but was finally persuaded to have some *bouillon*. However, despite having eaten next to nothing in the last few days, she ate no more than a few spoonfuls.

Under the gaze of her jailers, she dressed at 8 A.M., in a simple white dress—she had not been allowed to wear her black widow's dress in prison. She put on a linen cap with pleated edges and added two streamers and some black crepe to it, making it into a widow's bonnet. On her legs she wore black silk stockings and on her feet, plum-colored shoes.

Charles Henri Sanson, the executioner, came to her cell to cut off her hair and her hands were bound while she protested that her husband had not been bound. She had to be untied almost immediately to relieve herself, squatting humiliatingly in a corner of the cell.

Her procession to the scaffold in the Place de la Concorde began that morning at eleven o'clock. The day was fine, if a little misty, and she was put in a horse-drawn cart, seated with her back to the horses. Huge crowds lined the route and the painter David drew her from a window as she passed while the crowd screamed and spat at her. Marie Antoinette sat in her cart, "dignified and composed," to those of one camp, and "haughty and arrogant," to those of the other.

Arriving at the Place de la Concorde, she stepped down from the cart and is reported to have sprung up the steps to the scaffold, stopping, incredibly, to apologize to her executioner for treading on his toes.

Her head was chopped off by Madame Guillotine at 12:15 P.M. and held high by Sanson while the crowd rejoiced.

THE FUNERAL

Marie Antoinette's body was taken to the graveyard off the Rue d'Anjou, where her husband had been buried. The gravediggers had lunch before burying her, the head and body lying unattended on the grass. Madame Tussaud sculpted her face in melted wax while she lay there.

The bill for the funeral was six livres (around $24) for the coffin, and 15 livres and 35 sous (around $60) for the labor.

POST MORTEM

Marie Antoinette's last letter never reached Madame Elisabeth. It was given to Robespierre and only surfaced in 1816. It is now in the Archives Nationales.

✠

The few effects of this woman, who had once filled the palace of Versailles with her belongings, were distributed to the women of the Saltpêtrière Prison. They consisted of a few linen chemises, corsets in fine toile, two pairs of black stockings, a lawn headdress, some black crepe, some handkerchiefs, garters, and two pairs of cotton pockets in which she carried her belongings. There was also a box of powder, a sponge, and a little box of pomade. Four years later an auction was held of other effects—a small green morocco sewing box and three small portraits. They raised ten francs, 15 centimes.

✠

News of her death was received joyously throughout France

✠

Her son, Louis Charles XVII died of tuberculosis in 1795, age ten. There are no direct descendents of Marie Antoinette alive today.

✠

The remains of Marie Antoinette and Louis were exhumed in 1815 and removed to the cathedral of St. Denis, the traditional resting place of the Bourbons.

By Saturday, February 4, 1587, Mary Queen of Scots had been a prisoner for 19 years. In 1568, deeply unpopular with her nobles and her people, she had finally abdicated in favor of her son, James VI, and had crossed the Solway, the river that marked the border between Scotland and England, seeking the protection of the English queen. Elizabeth saw her as a threat, however, and, not knowing what to do with her, kept her a permanent prisoner in a succession of English strongholds.

Several plots against Queen Elizabeth had been discovered over the years, none of which seemed to directly involve Mary, but one, masterminded by Anthony Babington, finally implicated her through letters in which she apparently approved Elizabeth's death. As a result, she had been brought to trial in 1586 and sentenced to death. Elizabeth had not signed the death warrant until 1587 but it was by no means certain that she intended it to be carried out.

On that Saturday, when Mary's physician, Bourgoing, was given an evasive response to a simple request to go out to neighboring villages in search of herbal remedies, Mary became suspicious. The arrival of the Earls of Kent and Shrewesbury on Tuesday, February 7 did little to allay her fears. She began to realize that she would probably have no further need of remedies in this life.

She was given little time to prepare for her death. After dinner on February 7, the two newly arrived earls and the two custodians of the castle requested a meeting with her. Already in bed, she got up, dressed, and received them in her room.

Shrewesbury informed her that she had been condemned to death and the warrant was read out to her. Mary remained calm, replying that she would be happy to shed her blood for her church. She swore on a copy of the New Testament that she was innocent of all the crimes of which she had been found guilty.

Her devout Catholicism meant that she refused the offer of the services of the Protestant Dean of Peterborough to help her prepare for her end, and they would not allow her own chaplain to be admitted. She was told she would be executed at eight o'clock the following morning.

Her last evening was spent surrounded by her servants. She asked them to serve her supper quickly, as she had to put her affairs in order. She ate little and at the end of the meal, she asked her servants to raise their glasses to her. She then divided her money between them, personally writing each of their names on the packets. Mementos were put aside for royalty and for her relatives. Then she drew up a will in which she further provided for her staff, named the executors of her estate, and asked for requiem masses to be said in France after her death. She confessed her sins in a letter to her priest, the Chaplain de Préau, and, finally, wrote to her brother-in-law, King Henri of France.

By this time it was two in the morning and she lay down on her bed, fully dressed, her women gathered around her, all dressed in black. As the night echoed to the sound of hammering from the great hall where her scaffold was being erected, one of the servants read from the Bible.

February 8 dawned bright and sunny, and Mary rose at six to give each of her women a farewell embrace. She then went, alone, to pray and have some bread and wine.

Between eight and nine, a messenger arrived saying that the lords were ready for her. Mary finished her prayers and bade farewell to her servants—Elizabeth had ordered that she had to die alone. Speaking to them for the last time, Mary is reported to have said, "Tell my friends that I died a true Scottish woman and a true French woman." However, after pleading with the lords, she was finally permitted to take six of her women into the great hall with her.

The hall was filled with around three hundred spectators, a huge fire blazing in the large fireplace. A wooden stage about 12 feet square and two feet high had been constructed and hung with black. On the stage there were two stools, one each for Shrewesbury and Kent. Beside them was a small, cushioned stool on which the queen was to sit while her outer garments were being removed. The ax stood there and to the side of the stage were more seats for dignitaries and a rank of soldiers. Behind them stood the ordinary people who had been admitted.

Mary entered in silence, dressed entirely in black, except for a long, white, lace-edged veil and a white, peaked headdress, also edged with lace. Her satin dress was embroidered with black velvet and had black acorn buttons of jet, trimmed with pearl. Inner sleeves of purple were visible through the slashed sleeves of her dress and, contrasting with her shoes of black Spanish leather, were stockings decorated with silver. Her garters were of green silk and her petticoat was of crimson velvet. She held a crucifix and a prayer book in her hand and two rosaries dangled from her waist. Her stooping figure had grown full with age.

She was led up the steps to the stage and, still showing no emotion, listened while the warrant for her execution was read out. When the dean of Peterborough knelt in prayer, Mary turned from him and started to say her own prayer in Latin. When he had finished, she prayed out loud for the Church of England, for her son, and for the queen. She kissed the crucifix she held in her hand and ended by crossing herself and asking for her sins to be forgiven.

As was the custom, the executioners asked for forgiveness in advance. Then, helped by two of her servants, they undressed the queen. She was left wearing a red petticoat and a red bodice, the neckline—considerately for the executioners—cut low at the back. One of her women handed her a pair of red sleeves and she was ready to die, clad entirely in red, the color of blood and the liturgical color of martyrdom in Catholicism.

The executioners stretched out their hands for the queen's ornaments—a perk of the job—but there were protests when they tried to take her rosary and they were told that they would receive money instead.

Her lifelong servant, Jane Kennedy, bound Mary's eyes with the white cloth embroidered in gold that Mary had chosen, kissing it first and wrapping it around her head like a turban. Only her neck was left bare.

The queen, still showing no fear, knelt down on the cushion

in front of the block, reciting aloud a psalm in Latin. She laid her head on the block, placing her chin carefully with both hands. One of the executioners had to lean forward and move them as they were in the line of the ax's descent. She stretched out her legs and arms and cried out: *"In manus tuas, Domine, confide spiritum meum"*—"Into your hands, O Lord, I commend my spirit"— three or four times. The assistant to Bull, the executioner, put his hand on her body to steady it for the blow.

Bull missed with his first blow, merely cutting into the back of Mary's head. Her lips moved and her servants reported that they heard her utter the words "Sweet Jesus." The next blow severed the neck and it hung by a sinew that was cut using the ax as a saw.

Bull picked the head up and held it aloft, crying out "God Save the Queen!" Mary's lips were still moving and did so for a quarter of an hour after her death. As he held the head, the auburn tresses came away from it and the head fell to the ground. Her hair underneath was gray and very short.

It was ten o'clock in the morning of Wednesday, February 8. Mary Queen of Scots had died at age 44 and had chosen to meet her maker wearing a wig.

THE FUNERAL

Mary was entombed at Peterborough Cathedral. Elizabeth spent £321 on the funeral to placate Mary's son, King James of Scotland.

In 1612, a few years after becoming King of England and Scotland, James had her coffin removed to its final resting place in Westminster Abbey.

POST MORTEM

Fearing that relics could be created with them, Mary's heart and other organs were removed and burned that afternoon. Her body was then wrapped in a wax winding sheet and incarcerated in a heavy lead coffin.

On being told of the execution, Elizabeth was outraged. She had her secretary, William Davidson, thrown in prison for using the warrant, even though she had signed it. She insisted that she had only signed it "for safety's sake." In London, however, bells were rung and there was widespread celebration that the great threat of Mary Queen of Scots had been removed once and for all.

In France there was an outbreak of national mourning at the news of the dowager queen's demise and a requiem mass was held in a black-draped Notre Dame.

Meanwhile, Philip of Spain conveniently allowed himself to believe that Mary had disinherited her son James on the eve of her execution and had ceded her claims to the English throne to him. The next year, 1588, he made the momentous decision to pursue his supposed English inheritance with the great force of the Spanish Armada.

MARILYN MONROE

Marilyn Monroe's death remains one of Tinseltown's greatest mysteries, fueled by conflicting stories and persistent rumors. Did she take her own life in a haze of pills or was she murdered because she knew enough to ruin reputations at the highest levels?

Sadly, much of the evidence and testimony obtained during the investigation—including police files and interviews—has been lost or destroyed. Therefore, writing about the death of Marilyn can really only be speculative. However, there is certainly a great deal to be speculative about.

Here are just two of many versions of the last hours of the woman who was perhaps Hollywood's greatest star.

VERSION I

It was Saturday, August 4, 1962, and as usual, Marilyn had not slept well. Pat Newcomb, her press agent, had stayed the night at the house in Brentwood and upon waking at noon, found the star in a bad mood. "I had been able to sleep and Marilyn hadn't," said Newcomb later in an interview. "When I came out looking refreshed, it made her furious."

Marilyn spent a large part of the afternoon with her psychiatrist, Dr. Ralph Greenson, who had arrived just after lunch, following a phone call from the house asking if there was any oxygen available. She interrupted her consultation only to go for a drive with Eunice Murray, her assistant, who had arrived early that morning and was to spend much of the day there.

By this time it was obvious that Marilyn had swallowed one or more of the Nembutal barbiturate tablets prescribed to her the previous day by Dr. Hyman Engelberg. Dr. Greenson had been trying to break her Nembutal habit, switching her to chloral hydrate to help her sleep. Nembutal, however, was her drug of choice and she had a number of sources for it as well as a plentiful supply of capsules hidden around the house.

Around 5:30 P.M. Greenson asked Pat Newcomb to leave the house as Marilyn seemed unhappy having her around, speaking sharply to her several times. Not long after, around seven, the doctor also left.

Fifteen minutes or so later, Marilyn received a phone call from her ex-husband, Joe DiMaggio. He had gotten engaged but had decided to break off the engagement and wanted to talk to Marilyn about it. He later claimed that she seemed in good spirits when he talked to her, a view confirmed by Eunice Murray. Immediately after the call, Marilyn phoned Dr. Greenson to tell him about the broken engagement and he, like the others, thought she sounded fine.

Half an hour later, the actor Peter Lawford called to invite her to a party. But by this time her mood was radically different. She sounded heavily drugged and, he claims, seemed suicidal. He said that he shouted her name into the phone a few times when she didn't respond to his conversation. She is reported to have said, in a line that could have been taken from one of her films: "Say goodbye to Pat, say goodbye to the president, and say goodbye to yourself, because you're a nice guy." Lawford panicked and called his friend Milt Ebbins who, in turn, called Marilyn's lawyer, Milton Rudin. He convinced Rudin that he should go round to her house to check on her condition.

Instead of going to the house, however, Rudin called Eunice at around 8:30 P.M., asking her to check on the star. She did so and called back saying Marilyn was fine. Still not satisfied, however, Lawford put in a call at around 11 P.M. to another friend, Joe Naar, who lived close to Marilyn. He agreed to go over to the house to check that she had not overdosed but just as he was leaving, Rudin called, telling him not to bother. He said that Marilyn had been given a sedative by Dr. Greenson.

Eunice woke up around 3 A.M. and claims she saw a light under Marilyn's bedroom door (this claim is suspicious as the carpet's thick pile meant that nothing could be seen under the door). She claimed the door was locked (also suspicious as there was no working lock on the door), and she immediately called Dr. Greenson.

Greenson got into Marilyn's room at around 3:50 A.M. and found her dead on her bed.

VERSION 2

Another version of the story places Norman Jeffries, Eunice's son-in-law, at the house that night. According to him, between 9:30 and 10 P.M. the Attorney General Robert Kennedy, with whom Marilyn had been having an affair, arrived at the house with two other men. They ordered him and Eunice from the house and they went to the house of a neighbor, returning at around 10:30 P.M. when Kennedy and the two men left.

Jeffries claims that when they returned to the house, he saw Marilyn lying face down on her bed, naked and holding a telephone. He said she looked dead and Eunice called an ambulance and then the doctor.

Jeffries says that Peter Lawford and Pat Newcomb then arrived at the scene, shocked and hysterical. They summoned help. Ambulance driver Ken Hunter claims to have arrived in the early hours to find her in a coma. She was taken to Santa Monica Hospital where she died. The suggestion is that her body was then returned to her house to facilitate a cover-up.

Another eyewitness account supported Jeffries's claims, but it was never included in the records of the investigation into Marilyn's death. A neighbor told police that she saw Robert Kennedy and the two men approach Marilyn's house at about 6 or 7 P.M., carrying a black medical case. Although police refused to give any credence to her story, it was backed up by several other people who were playing cards with the neighbor. They all say they saw Bobby Kennedy drive up that evening.

Another phone call missing from some accounts is one Marilyn is said to have made to her hairdresser, Sydney Guilaroff, around 8:30 P.M. Guilaroff says that in a rambling conversation, Marilyn claimed to know a lot of dangerous secrets about the Kennedys and in another unrecorded call, to her sometime lover José Bolaños, she is said to have revealed "something shocking to him that would shock the whole world." As they spoke, she suddenly put down the phone without hanging up because she thought she had heard a disturbance at her front door. He never heard from her again.

THE FUNERAL

Marilyn's funeral service was held at Westwood Memorial Park, three days after her death. Joe DiMaggio made the arrangements, and only 31 close friends and relatives were invited. More than fifty Los Angeles police officers were at the cemetery, assisted by forty security guards hired by 20th Century Fox. Stands were set up outside the north wall of the cemetery to accommodate the press, and hundreds of fans stood quietly outside the cemetery gates.

DiMaggio had invited the poet Carl Sandburg to speak at the service, but he was ill and could not attend. The eulogy was delivered by her acting coach, Lee Strasberg. None of Marilyn's costars or friends from the entertainment industry were invited, even though many flew to Los Angeles to attend the funeral. "We could not in good conscience ask one personality to attend without perhaps offending many, many others," DiMaggio said. Privately, however, he blamed the film and entertainment community for his ex-wife's death.

Marilyn was buried in an $800 coffin, wearing a simple chartreuse Pucci dress, with a green scarf tied around her neck. In her hands was a tiny bouquet of baby pink roses, placed there by DiMaggio. After the service, just before the coffin was closed, DiMaggio leaned over, kissed Monroe on the lips and whispered, "I love you, I love you." That evening, after the funeral service was completed and Monroe's body had been placed in the crypt, he returned to the cemetery alone for a final, private farewell.

POST MORTEM

The coroner determined that Marilyn died from an overdose of barbituates. The drug pentobarbital (sleeping pills) was found in her liver and chloral hydrate was found in her blood. It was reported that there was no distinguishable physical evidence of foul play. The death was listed as a "probable suicide."

For the next twenty years, until 1983, DiMaggio arranged to have six red roses sent to Monroe's crypt three times a week. And when DiMaggio himself died in March 1999, his last words were reported to be, "I'll finally get to see Marilyn."

As her body was being prepared at the funeral home, someone observed that it didn't look like Marilyn Monroe because she was too flat-chested. The autopsy had left her like that but the family had provided a pair of breast-enhancers that Marilyn had worn occasionally. The falsies were removed from the dress, and a version of the most famous chest in the world was created using cotton wool.

THE CONSPIRACY THEORY

When Sergeant Jack Clemmons of the West Los Angeles Police Department arrived at the scene of Marilyn's death, at 4:25 P.M., he was led into the bedroom where he found her nude body covered with a sheet. "She was lying facedown in what I call the soldier's position. Her face was in a pillow, her arms were by her side, her right arm was slightly bent. Her legs were stretched out perfectly straight." His immediate thought was that she had been placed that way. He had seen a number of suicides and knew that an overdose of sleeping tablets usually causes victims to suffer convulsions and vomiting before they die in a contorted position. He continued, "Her hands were by her side and her legs were stretched out perfectly straight. It was the most obviously staged death scene I have ever seen. The pill bottles on her bedside table had been arranged in neat order and the body deliberately positioned. It all looked too tidy."

The statements of the three who were present seemed unusual to Clemmons. They claimed that Marilyn's body had been discovered some four hours earlier, but that they could not contact the police until 20th Century Fox's publicity department had given them permission.

There was no drinking glass in the bedroom to help Marilyn take the many pills that she was credited with swallowing.

The attendant who took Marilyn's body to the mortuary between 5:30 and 6 A.M. on Sunday morning noted that "rigor mortis was advanced," thus placing her time of death as between 9:30 and 11:30 P.M. on Saturday night.

Arthur Jacobs, Marilyn's publicist, was informed of Marilyn's death between 10 and 10:30 P.M. on Saturday.

The conclusions of the autopsy were disputed by some forensic experts who argued that there were no traces of Nembutal in Marilyn's stomach or intestinal tract. Also, there should have been specific crystals and evidence of the yellow capsules in which Nembutal is packaged. Not only were there no capsule parts, there was also no yellow dye from the capsules in her stomach.

Marilyn's biographer, Donald Spoto, contests that her blood count contained: "eight milligrams of chloral hydrate and four and a half milligrams of Nembutal, but in her liver there was a count of 13 milligrams, a much higher concentration of Nembutal. The ratio of Nembutal found in the blood compared to that in the liver suggested that Marilyn lived for many hours after the ingestion of that drug. This means that while Marilyn was alive and mobile throughout the day, the process of metabolizing the Nembutal she had taken had reached the liver and was beginning the process of excretion. The barbiturates were absorbed over a period of not minutes but hours. This report is consistent with what Greenson himself called her "somewhat drugged condition." This would rule out the suspicion of an injection of barbiturates. Plus, there were no needle marks and an injection of such an amount would cause immediate death. The only other way she could have ingested such an amount would be if they were administered in an enema, which would explain the "abnormal, anomalous discoloration of the colon." If this was indeed the method, it could only be the result of one of two things—an accident or murder.

Peter Lawford later claimed that Marilyn was an embarrassment to the Kennedys, especially in her ambitious aspirations to become the First Lady. Their rejection brought an enraged response from Marilyn. Hence her claim that she was in possession of information that would shake Jack Kennedy's presidency. It is very probable that she knew a lot about the president's involvement with Mafia head Sam Giancana and there would, in all likelihood, have been many other indiscretions. Did Bobby Kennedy arrive that night to announce to Marilyn that it was all over?

FBI tapes made that night are said to record an argument between Bobby and Marilyn. "Where is it? Where the fuck is it?" he is reported to be saying and "My family must have it," and "We'll make any arrangements you want," and "We'll pay you for it."

According to author Anthony Summers, Bobby Kennedy would have arrived to find Monroe overdosing but alive. An ambulance was called to take Marilyn to the hospital, but she died en route. Kennedy switched immediately to cover-up mode. According to Summers, the ambulance turned round and returned to the bungalow. The body was laid out on the bed, the room straightened, and a call placed to Robert Greenson. It was Greenson who officially discovered the dead Marilyn, by which time Bobby Kennedy was well away. A police officer pulled over a car driven by Peter Lawford sometime after midnight—hours after Marilyn died. Bobby Kennedy was in the back seat.

One rumor says that she was murdered by the Mafia, in revenge for Robert Kennedy's crusade against organized crime.

Marilyn was an inveterate diary-keeper. Lionel Grandison of the Los Angeles County Coroner's Office was the last person to have seen and examined Marilyn's red diary. He had sent his driver to Marilyn's house in the hope of recovering an address book so that relatives could be notified of Marilyn's death, but Eunice Murray gave the driver a little red diary as well as an address book. He stated that the diary contained references to the Kennedys and other people (notably Fidel Castro). Before leaving his office for the day, he locked it in the county coroner's office safe. When he returned to work on Tuesday, August 7, the safe was still locked but the diary was gone.

AHMAD SHAH MASSOUD

I n his book *The Soldiers of God,* Robert D. Kaplan describes Ahmad Shah Massoud as "one of the greatest leaders of guerrilla movements in the 20th century. He defeated his enemy just like Marshall Tito, Ho Chi Minh and Che Guevara did."

Meanwhile, *The Wall Street Journal* called him the "Afghan who won the cold war" because of the successes he had enjoyed during the Soviet occupation of his country. His troops had been the first mujahideen group to enter Kabul and he had helped establish a mujahideen government, in which he served as defense minister. When this government fell, the Taliban took over the capital and Massoud, with the help of Pakistan and his allies, withdrew to the north of the country, preventing the north and central regions from being taken. During this time, Massoud visited Paris and the European parliament to urge the world community to put pressure on Pakistan to stop supporting the Taliban and to deliver humanitarian aid to Afghanistan.

On September 8, 2001, just before al-Qaeda's attacks on New York, the "Lion of Panjshir," as he was known, met with 25 of his commanders in the northern Afghan town of Khaja Bahuddin, speaking by phone to other key figures in the Northern Alliance, the group of warlords he had galvanized against the Taliban.

His discussions finished, at around midnight he summoned his friend of twenty years, Khalili Massoud. As was his habit when he was exhausted and under great pressure, Massoud wanted to talk not about war, but about poetry and Sufi mysticism. Khalili was used to hearing Massoud say, "Poetry makes me peaceful, it makes me relax."

Massoud certainly had plenty to worry about. At that time, the Taliban controlled all but ten percent of the country and a massive attack was expected. Furthermore, the onset of the unforgiving Afghan winter was imminent. The influence of Osama bin Laden over the Taliban gave him further cause for alarm and persuaded him to ready his troops.

But on this September night, Massoud pushed all of that to the back of his mind and asked his old friend to read to him from the work of the Persian poet Hāfiz: "Open it; see what will come." The tradition says that a verse from Iran's most celebrated writer, chosen at random, shows what the future holds.

Khalili read: "This night we are talking together value it, because many days pass, many months go, many years come, you will not be able to find this night that we are together."

Massoud had agreed to grant an interview next day to two Arab journalists who had been waiting two days for their opportunity to meet him. He took Khalili with him as he wanted to accompany him to the Oxus River afterward for lunch and then travel on to the Panjshir Valley.

They sat in a room that they called the Afghan Foreign Ministry, Khalili seated to Massoud's right. The cameraman and journalist introduced themselves as Moroccans—although they were actually Tunisians—representing an Islamic center based in London, and they claimed to have traveled through the Taliban zone. The reporter read out the 15 questions he wanted to ask. Eight of them referred to bin Laden and this annoyed Massoud. However, he finally said, "OK, is the camera ready?"

"Yes," said the reporter, calmly and quietly. "What is the situation in Afghanistan?"

Khalili recalls seeing not the slightest worry in Massoud's eyes, but only the first word was translated when there was a huge explosion. Khalili was seriously hurt, his body riddled by hundreds of splinters, his heart protected by his passport, which Massoud had stuffed into his shirt pocket earlier.

Massoud however, was—in the words of another journalist—"a mess." His body was taken immediately by helicopter to Tajikistan where he died shortly after.

THE FUNERAL

Massoud was buried on the hill of Saricha in Panjshir. He had personally selected this place for his grave.

POST MORTEM

Posthumously, the Afghan interim government under President Karzai awarded Massoud the title "Hero of the Afghan Nation."

✠

Khalili is convinced that Massoud's death was instigated on the orders of bin Laden who foresaw the consequences of 9/11—a military campaign that would put an end to the Taliban. He reckons that Massoud's death was designed both to eliminate a potential U.S. ally and to please Mullah Omar, the leader of the Taliban. "Everyone knows they were sent by bin Laden," he says. "He ordered it personally."

MATA HARI

As was customary, the detachment of soldiers tried to be as noisy as possible as they marched along the corridor to the condemned woman's cell. The intention was to wake her up before their arrival, giving her the first indication that today was the day she would die. The authorities believed it inhumane to announce to the condemned person the date of his or her execution in advance.

But on this morning—October 15th, 1917—even the stamping of military boots on the hard, cold stone floor failed to wake Mata Hari, the internationally famous, exotic Dutch dancer and courtesan who had been found guilty of spying for Germany and sentenced to death by firing squad. She had taken a sedative the previous evening and its effects had not yet worn off.

She had made a last-minute plea for clemency from the French president, Raymond Poincaré, but as she was gently stirred from her deep sleep by the two nuns who had been attending her and saw her lawyer Maître Clunet and Bouchardon, the army captain who had interrogated her, she realized that her appeal had been rejected. "It's not possible!" she exclaimed, becoming overwrought. But the nuns comforted her and she calmed down. "Don't be afraid, Sister," she said to one in defiance, "I shall know how to die."

She asked to write two letters and was immediately provided with ink, pens, and stationery. Seated on the edge of her bed, she quickly wrote the letters, sealed them in the envelopes and gave them to her lawyer. She then pulled on a pair of black silk stockings and high-heeled shoes, fastening them with silk ribbons. Over the black silk kimono she was wearing over her nightdress, she placed a long, black velvet cloak, edged with fur and with a fur collar, wrapping it around her shoulders.

On her head, to cover the braided coils of her black hair, she put a large, black felt hat decorated with a ribbon and a bow. She then pulled on a pair of black kid gloves and without emotion said, "I am ready."

A car waited outside the prison to take her to the barracks where the execution was to take place. It was barely 5:30 in the morning and Paris was not yet awake as the vehicle sped along its wide boulevards to the Caserne de Vincennes.

On arriving at their destination, the party quickly descended from the vehicle, Mata Hari last, and walked immediately to the place of execution where 12 soldiers of a Zouave regiment stood at ease. Behind them stood an officer, his sword drawn.

They walked to a mound of earth, seven or eight feet tall, that would serve to stop any bullets that were not on target. A priest, Father Arbaux, spoke quietly to Mata Hari as an officer approached, a white cloth that was to serve as a blindfold fluttering from his hand. He handed it to one of the nuns.

"Must I wear that?" she asked her lawyer. He turned to the officer who replied that she did not have to, if she did not want to. The officer then turned hurriedly away. As the nuns and Maître Clunet moved away from her, she turned, unbound and not blindfolded, to look at her executioners. Each looked back, praying that his rifle contained the blank cartridge that had been placed in one of the weapons so that there would always be doubt as to who had actually killed her.

The officer issued a sharp command and the men came to attention. Another command rang out and they raised their rifles to their shoulders, taking careful aim. Mata Hari stood still. The officer moved into view of the firing squad and extended his sword in the air. After the briefest of moments, he dropped it and the soldiers squeezed their triggers, the sound of a dozen gunshots echoing around the barracks.

Mata Hari collapsed slowly to her knees, her head still held up, her expression unchanged. She gazed at the soldiers for a long moment and then slumped backwards, bending at the waist, her legs doubled up beneath her and her face turned towards the sky.

As was customary, one of the officers present walked toward her, drew his pistol and placed the barrel close to her left temple. He pulled the trigger, firing a single bullet into her brain, making sure that 41-year-old Mata Hari was dead.

She died as she had lived, however. In the moment before the Zouaves had pulled their triggers, she had blown them a last, memorable kiss.

THE FUNERAL

No one claimed Mata Hari's body, and she was not afforded the dignity of a funeral. Instead, her body was removed to a medical school where it was dissected to teach medical students.

POST MORTEM

After her death, Mata Hari's fame increased and she became something of a legend. Greta Garbo, Marlene Dietrich, Sylvia Kristel, and Jeanne Moreau have all portrayed her on film.

EVA PERON

She had been ill since 1950. A few days after Eva Perón had fainted while inaugurating a building in Buenos Aires, doctors had removed her appendix, but also discovered the real cause of her constant exhaustion and ill health—uterine cancer, ominously the disease that had killed the first wife of her husband, Argentina's President Juan Domingo Perón.

Now, two years later, she lay in a room in the presidential residence that was far enough away from his room to prevent him hearing her screams as she waited to die.

She had been born into poverty on May 7, 1922, as Eva Duarte, and her parents had never married. By the age of twenty she had moved to Buenos Aires and had begun to find success as an actress in films and on radio.

In 1944 she met Colonel Juan Perón, at the time working in the Argentinian Labor Department. Age did not deter them—he was 27 years older than her—and before long they had scandalized Buenos Aires society by moving in together. In 1946 he was elected president of Argentina, with Eva campaigning resolutely at his side. People, especially the poor, loved her passion and began to call her Evita, "Little Eva."

She created the Eva Perón Foundation, having diverted government funding for it from another organization, the Sociedad de Beneficencia, a group of well-to-do ladies who had unwisely snubbed her because of her humble origins. In the next few years she spent tens of millions of dollars helping the poor, building hospitals, schools, and old people's homes. She campaigned for and got the vote for Argentinian women and became idolized in her country.

In August 1951, Juan and Evita climbed onto a stage in Buenos Aires to be greeted by the hysterical demands of the huge crowd for Evita to stand as vice president in the forthcoming presidential elections. In a magnificent piece of theater, she agreed to comply with the will of the people. The military had other ideas, however, and bridled at the thought of a woman vice president who would be just a heart attack away from taking over for her husband and assuming command of the armed forces. Nine days after she had responded to the crowd's pleas, she withdrew her candidacy, fearing a military coup.

On October 17, an assembly was held to celebrate Evita's renunciation of her candidacy. Her husband delivered a eulogy to her and then she delivered a speech containing words that resonated with the Argentinian people: "I have left the shreds of my life on the road." On its conclusion, she collapsed into Juan's arms.

In September she was examined under general anesthetic at the President Perón Clinic, a facility built by her foundation. The surgeon was George Pack from the Memorial Sloan-Kettering Cancer Center in New York, but Evita was not told who he was or what her illness was. It was decided that she required a hysterectomy and in early November, Pack returned to carry out the procedure. Meanwhile, they hid from the outside world the true nature of her illness.

They removed her uterus and some lymph nodes, but

discovered with dismay that the cancer had spread. However, the prognosis following the operation was positive. A few days later, when the election took place, the first in which Argentinean women could exercise their right to vote, a ballot box was brought to her bedside. A photograph at the time shows her to be frail and thin. The writer David Viñas related later how as he took the ballot box containing her vote back, one woman knelt before him on the pavement and kissed it.

Perón won by a landslide and by Christmas, Eva was beginning to return to public life, giving a talk on the radio and distributing Christmas presents to poor children who had been brought to the residence. She began to meet with workers and ministers, but by February 1952, she was unwell again, the pain of her cancer returning and her weight loss becoming dramatic. Another biopsy revealed the further spread of the disease. They calculated that she had no more than a month to live.

But Evita was stronger than that. In early April, she attended the funeral of the man who had replaced her as vice presidential candidate, Hortensio Quijano, and the next day she read the manuscript of her autobiography. That same day, Prince Bernard of the Netherlands awarded her the Great Cross of the Orange-Nassau Order.

On May 1, she made her final speech. She was skeleton-thin, wearing a shapeless dress to disguise it. Juan held her up by the waist as the cheers of the huge crowd resounded around the square.

On June 4 she was still alive but weighed only 82 pounds and could barely stand. When Perón traveled to the building of the Congress of the Argentine Nation, standing up and waving in an open-topped car, she stood beside him. But a huge dose of morphine coursed through her veins and her fur coat hid the fact that a belt tied her to the window behind the driver. They had also created a plaster support for her. Through it all, she waved and smiled.

The country held masses for her, broadcast on national radio, but she was not allowed to listen as they persisted in lying to her about her condition. The newspapers she read were specially printed editions that excluded all mentions of her illness. Family and friends stayed with her in eight-hour shifts.

Finally, on June 18, she slipped into a coma. Once again, the doctors wrote her off but she awoke and, saying that she would die if she stayed in bed, incredibly, she got up.

On the night before she died, Perón visited her. He had had great trouble accepting what his once-beautiful wife had become in illness and had not been to look at her for two days.

The next day, Saturday, June 26, when her mother, Doña Juana, briefly left her room, Evita sighed to her sister, Elisa, "Poor old lady." Elisa replied that, on the contrary, their mother looked good. Evita replied, "I know. *Lo digo porque Eva se va.*" ("I say this because Eva is leaving.") These were the last words she would utter. She died at age 33.

The Funeral

There would be no funeral for Evita for a while.

Post Mortem

Spanish doctor Pedro Ara had been engaged to mummify

Evita's corpse. He went to work immediately, making her first of all, look good for her lying-in-state at the Ministry of Labor. Her hair was colored and styled in her customary chignon and her nails were manicured. Dressed in a white shroud and the Argentian flag, she was placed in a glass casket, rosary beads that had been given to her by the pope interwoven in her fingers. Lines formed, stretching for miles, and two people died as they waited in the rain. For 13 days they lined up to touch or kiss the casket. For three of those days the entire country had to wear a black tie or an armband. On August 9, she was borne on a gun carriage in front of an audience of two million on the wet streets of the capital to Congress and then to the building of the Argentinian Labor Confederation to await the construction of a huge monument that Juan had planned. There, Pedro Ara began his work, preserving her body for all time, as a kind of metaphor for Perónism.

The monument failed to materialize but it became immaterial when, in September 1955, Perón was overthrown and went into exile in Madrid, leaving Evita's preserved body behind. For a while, she remained with Ara before being taken by the army. She was supposed to be buried in a local cemetery but the officer in charge of her kept her. Following her discovery, she was taken secretly to Italy, where she was buried with another woman's name on the headstone in a cemetery in Milan. A letter containing details of her location was given to the new president, Pedro Aramburu, but he refused to open it, giving it to a lawyer and ordering him to pass it to the next president four weeks after his death.

✼

In 1970, former president Aramburu was taken from his home by two men in uniform and questioned about many things, including the location of Eva Perón's body. He told them only that the Vatican had supervised her burial and lied, saying that she was in Rome. He would say no more and for his obduracy he was executed. Four weeks after his death, the lawyer passed the letter to General Alexandro Lanusse, head of the Argentinian government at the time.

Her body was discovered and delivered in the back of a bakery truck to Perón in Madrid where he kept her in the attic of his home. The body was still in an astonishingly good condition, but there was damage to her nose and feet as well as gashes on her cheek and a finger missing.

In October 1973, Perón was miraculously returned to power. He had remarried and his new wife, Isabel, appeared on posters with him. But there was a third person on those posters and billboards—Evita. He lasted only nine months, however, before dying of a heart attack. Isabel took over the presidential reins.

On November 17, 1974, Eva Perón's body finally returned to Argentina. She was taken to Juan's Olivos residence and repair work was undertaken.

On March 26, 1976, during the overthrow of Isabel Perón by a military coup led by future president General Videla, Evita's body was ejected from the Olivos residence. In October of that year, the casket was returned to her family and she was finally laid to rest in the family vault in Buenos Aires' Recoleta cemetery, 24 years after her death.

RIVER PHOENIX

October 30, 1993 was just another day for handsome young film star River Phoenix. He spent much of it in front of the camera on a Hollywood soundstage, filming interior scenes for *Dark Blood*, in which he was playing a hermit living on a nuclear testing site, waiting for the end of the world. *Dark Blood* had marked a return to acting for Phoenix. A few years previously, he had become tired of the star machine, returning to live with his family in Florida and calling himself Rio. Now his career was back on track and he had just signed to star in a major production, *Interview with the Vampire*, alongside Tom Cruise.

When the cameras stopped rolling at around 7 P.M., River returned to his hotel, the Nikko. Waiting for him there were his actress girlfriend, Samantha Mathis, his sister Rain and his brother Joaquin. Before long the quartet were partying noisily. River was set that evening on heading to the Viper Room at 8852 West Sunset Boulevard, an infamous club frequented by celebrities and part-owned by another rising young film star, Johnny Depp. Even in the 1940s, the Viper Room had enjoyed a dubious reputation. As the Melody Room, it had been used by gangster Bugsy Siegel as an illicit gambling den.

Some friends of River were playing at the Viper Room that night—Flea, bass player of the Red Hot Chili Peppers; Al Jourgensen from Ministry; and Gibby Haynes of the Butthole

Surfers. At around 10 P.M. the group left the Nikko and traveled to the club by car. River was wearing a pair of striped brown trousers and black-and-white Converse high tops.

At 1 A.M., he was in the bathroom doing drugs when someone offered him a snort of high-grade heroin with the street name Persian Brown. He didn't say "No." Immediately, however, River began shaking uncontrollably and vomiting. Incredibly, some thought they were helping when they offered him a Valium.

The young actor staggered back out into the bar and found Samantha Mathis and Rain Phoenix. By this time, however, he was having difficulty breathing and briefly passed out. Coming to, he asked Mathis to take him outside but she first called River's friend and assistant, Abby, before she and Joaquin helped him out of the club. Outside, River collapsed on the pavement and began having seizures.

Ron Davis, a photographer waiting outside the club for celebrity photo opportunities, called 911 at the nearby pay-phone, as did Joaquin. "He looked like a fish out of water," Davis later said, describing how the actor was "thrashing spasmodically, his head flopping from side to side, arms flailing wildly."

Rain Phoenix emerged from the Viper Room, throwing herself on River in a desperate attempt to stop the seizures, but he suddenly became very still and stopped breathing. It was 1:14 A.M.

When paramedics arrived, River was in full cardiac arrest and Ray Ribar of the L.A. County Fire Department began to administer heart massage. The actor was put in the ambulance and rushed to Cedars-Sinai Medical Center, arriving at 1:34 A.M.

On arrival, River's skin was dark blue, but his body was still warm. For twenty frantic minutes, the ER doctors fought to revive him, even inserting a pacemaker, but he was pronounced dead at 1:51 A.M. on October 31, 1993, just 23 years old.

The Funeral

River, wearing a black T-shirt with the logo of his band Aleka's Attic, was placed in a blue coffin for a viewing on November 4 at the Milam Funeral Home. His normally blond shoulder-length hair, dyed black for *Dark Blood*, was cut by the mortician and, at the request of Heart Phoenix, River's mother, it was placed beside him in the coffin. Heart placed a single carnation in the casket and many of the sixty mourners also left items such as notes and necklaces.

After his cremation, his ashes remained in the care of his family. A memorial service, held on the Paramount Studios lot on November 18, was attended by Sidney Poitier, Rob Reiner, Richard Benjamin, John Boorman, and Peter Bogdanovich.

Post Mortem

The official cause of River Phoenix's death was acute multiple drug ingestion. The autopsy showed lethal levels of cocaine and morphine (heroin shows up as morphine as the body metabolizes it), Valium, marijuana, and ephedrine. Ephedrine is the main ingredient found in crystal meth.

✚

The telephone call made by Joaquin Phoenix, calling the emergency services, was aired repeatedly in the media over the days following his brother's death. "You must get here, please, because he's dying," he screams in desperation.

✠

Married With Children star Christina Applegate was at the club that night and witnessed the seizures, which she later reenacted as an anti-drug dance piece.

PABLO PICASSO

Diego José Santiago Francisco de Paula Juan Nepomuceno Crispín Crispiniano de los Remedios Cipriano de la Santísima Trinidad Ruiz Blasco y Picasso López—a.k.a Pablo Picasso—once told a friend. "Death holds no fear for me. It has a kind of beauty. What I am afraid of is falling ill and not being able to work. That's lost time."

On April 7, 1973, Picasso was, as usual, losing no time. Despite having been laid low with a bad bout of influenza the previous winter, the ninety-year-old artist was hard at work in Notre-Dame-de-Vie, his hilltop villa at Mougins on the French Riviera, preparing for the following month's exhibition in Avignon of two hundred examples of his recent work. Of course, Picasso no longer had any need for money or the blandishments of critics. These days, he was in competition only with himself and the great works of his life.

As was his custom in the late afternoon sunshine, he went for a stroll in the little park surrounding the sprawling stone house with its view of the foothills of the Maritime Alps. There, he would sometimes gather flowers and vegetables and take them into his studio to draw them. Jacques Barra, Picasso's gardener, recalls: "That day I showed him the anemones and pansies, which he particularly liked."

In the evening, Picasso and his wife Jacqueline had some friends over for dinner. Picasso, in high spirits, urged the guests to "Drink to me; drink to my health! You know I can't drink any more."

At 11:30 P.M., he stood up from the table, declaring that he had to go back to work. He remained in his studio, painting until 3 A.M.

The next day, Sunday, April 8, Picasso awoke as usual at 11:30, but was unable to get out of bed. Jacqueline and his son, Paolo, immediately summoned help, but just ten minutes later, before a doctor could get there, the twentieth century's greatest artist had a heart attack and died.

THE FUNERAL

Picasso was interred at the park at Castle Vauvenargues, in Vauvenargues, Bouches-du-Rhône. Jacqueline prevented his children Claude and Paloma from attending the funeral.

POST MORTEM

Picasso's death was attributed to a heart attack brought on by pulmonary edema, fluid in the lungs.

✠

At the time of his death Picasso was a multi-millionaire who owned a vast quantity of his own work, consisting of personal favorites that he had kept off the art market. He also had a considerable collection of the work of many other famous artists, such as Henri Matisse, with whom he had exchanged works. Since he had left no will, his death duties were paid in kind, in the form of works by him and others from his collection. These constitute the core of the immense and representative collection at the Musée Picasso in Paris.

In 2003 his relatives inaugurated a museum dedicated to him
in his birthplace, Malága—the Museo Picasso Malága.

Jacqueline Roque, Picasso's second wife, shot herself
13 years after Picasso's death.

SYLVIA PLATH

As 1962 faded into 1963, Britain seemed to be covered by a sheet of ice. It was the worst winter in sixty years, and thirty-year-old Sylvia Plath and her children, Frieda and Nicholas, had been suffering from flu. Living in a second-floor flat at 23 Fitzroy Road, Primrose Hill, Sylvia was experiencing violent mood swings and was undergoing treatment for depression. She was struggling to cope and had hired a Belgian au pair, but the girl lasted less than a month.

At the end of the first week of February, Sylvia's doctor, Dr. Horder, was becoming concerned. She was thin and anxious and her sleeping pills were no longer working. Additionally, her depression was not being eased by the new medication he had prescribed. He tried unsuccessfully to find her a hospital bed for the weekend so she ended up at a friend's house, railing against her estranged husband, the poet Ted Hughes, for his infidelity, and depressed by the indifference of American reviewers to her novel *The Bell Jar*.

She returned home on February 10, claiming that she was feeling better. But when she went down to the flat of a neighbor at 11:45 P.M. to buy some stamps from him, he thought she looked very ill and suggested calling a doctor. She refused and they said goodnight. Ten minutes after he had closed the door, however, he opened it again and Sylvia was still standing there. Again she refused his pleas to contact her doctor, saying that she was having a vision or a dream. For the rest of the night he heard her pacing the floor above his head.

Some time early in the morning of February 11, Sylvia made careful preparations. She placed bread and cups of milk beside her children's beds, opened their windows wide, and stuffed the cracks under the bedroom and kitchen doors with towels. She had already consumed a quantity of sleeping pills and had written a note asking that her doctor be called.

Around nine, a nurse who visited her daily became concerned that her knocks at the door were going unanswered. She found a builder who gained entrance and in the kitchen, they found Sylvia's body. She had knelt beside the open gas oven and turned on the gas.

She had already had one go at suicide while attending Smith College in her home town of Boston. This time it worked.

THE FUNERAL

Sylvia Plath was buried on February 16, 1963, in Heptonstall Cemetery, West Yorkshire, close to the Hughes family home, under the name "Sylvia Plath Hughes." The inscription reads: "Even amidst fierce flames / The golden lotus can be planted."

POST MORTEM

On February 17, 1963, the critic Al Alvarez wrote
a memorial essay in the *The New York Observer*
about Plath, "A Poet's Epitath," in which he eulogized:
"The loss to literature is inestimable."

✠

In 1965, *Ariel*, the collection of forty poems she had written
in the months before her death, was published. By 1968
more than eight thousand hardcovers and twenty thousand
paperbacks had been sold in the UK alone. Further collections
followed in coming years and all sold phenomenally well.

Six years after Sylvia's death, Assia Wevill, the woman who
had lured Ted Hughes away from Plath, killed herself and their
four-year-old daughter Shura in exactly the same way
that Sylvia did.

Hughes was vilified for years after Sylvia's suicide, especially
by feminists. Often, his readings were disrupted by women
bearing banners declaring him a murderer.

The name "Hughes" has on many occasions
been scratched off Sylvia's tombstone.

EDGAR ALLAN POE

The misery of Edgar Allan Poe's life is matched only by the mystery of his death.

His young wife, Virginia, whom he had married in 1835 when she was only 13, had died of tuberculosis in the early 1840s and Poe had become increasingly unstable. Although he had achieved a measure of success with his poem "The Raven," published in 1845, it had failed to make him and he had earned a paltry nine dollars from its publication. The precarious nature of his professional life as a writer and magazine editor, coupled with the stress of Virginia's illness and early death, had increased his already heavy drinking.

Poe had been living in a cottage in the Bronx and had become engaged to the poet, essayist, and spiritualist Sarah Helen Whitman. But she began to tire of his erratic behavior and frequent drunkenness. In 1848 for instance, when he was traveling to visit Sarah in Providence, he took an overdose of laudanum and almost died. He eventually took a vow to remain sober during their engagement, but no sooner had he taken the vow than it was broken. To make matters worse, Sarah's mother was set against him marrying her daughter and she accused him of pursuing two other women while engaged to her daughter. The relationship ended.

He had been in Richmond, Virginia, visiting Sarah Elmira Royster, a former childhood sweetheart with whom he was attempting to rekindle a relationship, and on September 27, he took a train from Richmond to New York. No more was heard of him until October 3 when a printer by the name of Joseph W. Walker found him seated on a wooden plank outside Ryan's Tavern on Lombard Street in Baltimore. Poe was delirious, unwashed, and shabbily dressed, uncharacteristic of a man normally fairly punctilious about his appearance. The doctor who attended to him, John Joseph Moran, later said he was wearing a stained and faded woolen jacket, dirty trousers, an old straw hat, and a pair of down-at-the-heels worn-out shoes.

The writer was transported in a carriage to Washington College Hospital in Baltimore, where he was put in a wing of the hospital with bars on the windows. This area was reserved for people who were ill from drinking, although Moran quickly realized that Poe was not drunk. He was incoherent for much of the time, uttering the name "Reynolds" repeatedly. In his delirium he was unable to tell them how he came to be in this state on a street in Baltimore, apparently dressed in someone else's clothes, and Dr. Moran surmised that he had been robbed and his clothing had been stolen.

When asked about his friends, Moran claims that Poe said, "My best friend would be the man who gave me a pistol that I might blow out my brains." He referred to a wife, possibly forgetting in his feverish condition that Virginia was dead.

At five in the morning on October 7, Edgar Allan Poe is said to have uttered the words, "Lord help my poor soul," and died, at age forty.

The Funeral

Poe was buried in the grounds of Westminster Hall and Burial Ground in a simple ceremony at 4 P.M. on Monday, October 8, 1849, in a cheap mahogany coffin paid for by his uncle Henry Herring. It lacked handles, a nameplate, a cloth lining, and a cushion for his head. The hearse was paid for by his cousin, Neilson Poe, and his shroud was made by the wife of Dr. Moran. The mourners were Poe's friend Dr. Joseph Snodgrass, a former University of Virginia classmate, and Poe's cousin, Elizabeth Herring, and her husband. It was a damp, bitter cold day and the Reverend W.T.D. Clemm, a cousin of Poe's late wife, decided to dispense with a sermon in view of the cold and the small number of mourners. The proceedings lasted a mere three minutes.

Post Mortem

A white Italian marble headstone planned for the grave and paid for by Neilson Poe was destroyed when a train derailed and crashed into the yard where it was being stored. Consequently, his grave was marked by a piece of sandstone on which was inscribed "No. 80." In 1873, following a visit to Poe's grave, the poet Paul Hamilton Hayne wrote a newspaper article suggesting a better monument. Money was raised in Baltimore and throughout the United States and a monument which cost little more than $1,500 was designed and built. It included a medallion of Poe by an artist named Valck. On October 1, 1875, his body was exhumed and reinterred close to the entrance to the church. At a dedication ceremony on November 17, Neilson Poe described his cousin as "one of the best-hearted men that ever lived." The poet Walt Whitman was the only one of the poets invited who attended, although Alfred Lord Tennyson contributed a poem that was read.

✠

The cause of Poe's death has been the subject of speculation for the more than one hundred-fifty years since his death, mainly because his death certificate and medical reports have all been lost, if, indeed, they ever existed. There are countless theories as to what killed him, including a rare brain disease, a brain tumor, diabetes, enzyme deficiencies, syphilis, heart disease, epilepsy, and meningitis. The newspapers of the day attributed it to "congestion of the brain" or "cerebral inflammation," both of which were simply euphemisms used at the time to disguise the disgrace of a death from alcoholism. In 2006, hairs from Poe's head were analyzed and found not to contain heavy amounts of lead or mercury, thus discounting poisoning. Rabies was recently added to the list as well as cholera—he had been in Philadelphia in the winter of 1849 when a cholera epidemic had been raging. His friend Dr. Snodgrass attributed his death to alcoholism and, being a passionate supporter of the temperance movement, used Poe as an example of the evil that can be done by the demon drink. This theory was refuted, however, in 1885 by Joseph Moran who said that Poe did not smell of alcohol when he brought him into the hospital. Others say that Poe was not a great drinker unless under undue stress, and one claimed that he would get drunk on just one glass of wine.

✚

When he died, he was a member of the Sons of Temperance.

✚

Poe's drug habit is also disputed. A doctor friend said that if
Poe had been an opium user, as has been claimed,
he would have seen signs of it and he did not.

✚

One suggestion as to his cause of death is that he was a victim of the illegal practice of "cooping," in which unwilling
people were kidnapped and "cooped" up in places where they
were drugged or forced to drink whiskey until they did not
know what they were doing. On election day, they were carried around and forced to vote in numerous wards. It was
election day when Poe was found and he did repeat the name
"Reynolds"; one of the judges overseeing the Fourth Ward polls
at Ryan's Tavern was called Reynolds.

✚

Poe's image as a drug-addled drunk was created by one man—
Rufus Wilmot Griswold, a well-known poet, editor, and critic.
He disliked Poe intensely and the character assassination he
carried out on him before his death was perpetuated after it.
Writing as "Ludwig," he provided a bizarrely unpleasant obituary. He wrote of Poe walking the streets "in madness or melan-
choly, with lips moving in indistinct curses," and described him
as a "brilliant, but erratic star." Unfortunately, Poe's character as
described by Griswold, both in the obituary and in a biographical piece in a collection of Poe's work, became the accepted
view of the writer. Readers became titillated by the thought

of reading the work of a depraved character who resembled in many ways the characters he created.

✚

Many have tried to identify the owner of the name "Reynolds" that Poe shouted out a number of times as he lay dying. Some have suggested Jeremiah N. Reynolds, who was a newspaper editor and explorer and may have provided the inspiration for Poe's 1838 novel, *The Narrative of Arthur Gordon Pym of Nantucket*. Others claim that it must have been Judge Henry R. Renolds (see above).

✚

Edgar Allan Poe has been credited since his death with inventing detective fiction as well as science fiction. The annual awards given by the Mystery Writers of America are known as the Edgars.

✚

An essay written by Poe in 1848, "Eureka: A Prose Poem," describes the Big Bang Theory a full eighty years before it was scientifically proven. He also made influential contributions to cryptography and cosmology.

✚

Every year since 1949, a mystery visitor has toasted Poe's memory at his graveside. Every year, on January 19, the man known as the "Poe Toaster" visits the grave in the early hours of the morning, toasts him with cognac, and leaves three roses.

ELVIS PRESLEY

The Elvis Presley of 1977 was a very different person than the young lion who had exploded onto the music scene in Memphis more than twenty years previously, rewriting the rules of popular music and earning untold riches in the process. The Elvis of the late seventies was a sad, bloated figure who had overindulged in pharmaceuticals and junk food for too long and whose stage performances were becoming increasingly sloppy and embarrassing.

On Monday, August 15, 1977, he was preparing to leave his Memphis home, Graceland, two days later for Portland, Maine, where he was due to launch a short tour. As usual, he woke at around four in the afternoon and three hours later, sent for his cousin Billy Smith. In his daily life Elvis lived in a cocoon of sorts, surrounded by a coterie of friends and relatives who hovered around him like bees around a honeypot. He expected these people to play according to his rules, however, and as they fed off him, it could be said that to a certain extent he fed off them, too.

For years, Elvis would wake up in the late afternoon to begin his day. He would play racquetball, hire movie theaters and fun parks, and live his life when the rest of the world was asleep. And he expected his friends to do the same—the women in his life and the so-called Memphis Mafia, consisting of boyhood friends and cousins who had been with him all the way on the fabulous ride that had been his career.

On this particular Monday, he wanted to arrange a screening of the film *MacArthur*, starring Gregory Peck. Ricky Stanley, Elvis's stepbrother—his father, Vernon, had remarried after the death of Elvis's beloved mother, Gladys—was charged with organizing the screening, but the cinema could not find a print of the film so Elvis and Billy elected to just watch television.

Elvis had an appointment arranged with his dentist, Dr Hoffman, for 10:30 P.M. (even his physicians and dentists had to work on "Elvis time"), and asked Billy to call his girlfriend, Ginger Alden. He had first met 21-year-old Ginger the previous November when she came out to visit the house with her sister, Terry, the reigning Miss Tennessee. Everyone had thought Elvis would go for Terry, but it was only Ginger he had eyes for.

Dressed in a black Drug Enforcement Agency sweatsuit, with two .45 revolvers stuffed in the waistband of his trousers, he left by the back stairs, accompanied by Ginger, Charlie, and his cousin, Joe Esposito. Due to Elvis's swollen ankles, the zips on his black leather boots remained undone.

The dentist cleaned Elvis's teeth and filled a couple of small cavities. He talked about his daughter with Dr. Hoffman who, like Elvis, had a daughter out in California. Jokingly, the singer suggested that at the conclusion of his tour they should fly out on Elvis's jet, the *Lisa Marie*, and surprise the girls.

The party returned to Graceland soon after midnight in good spirits. Elvis's teeth felt fine, but he had made sure to get some codeine tablets just in case. He then went upstairs alone, calling down to Joe with some last-minute tour instructions and also making arrangements for his visiting daughter to be flown back to California on a commercial flight.

Elvis and Ginger then picked up the threads of the argument they always had before a tour and once again she refused to fly out with him that night. But Elvis let it go and they talked instead, about what would be the best date to get married.

Dr. George Nichopoulos, known as Dr. Nick, had been Elvis's personal physician for some years and he was not surprised to receive a call from the singer at 2:15 A.M. Elvis was having a little pain from one of the teeth that had been filled earlier and needed some painkillers. Ricky Stanley was sent out to the all-night pharmacy to pick up a prescription for six Dilaudid tablets.

All was quiet then until four in the morning when Billy and Jo received a call from Elvis asking if they wanted to play racquetball with him. On the way to the racquetball building it was raining and when Billy said he was sick of the rain, Elvis retorted, "Ain't no problem. I'll take care of it." He held up his hands and, coincidentally, the rain stopped.

They played a few games, but Elvis, unfit and carrying too much weight, tired rapidly and it quickly deteriorated into a game of dodgeball. When Elvis hit his shin with his racket they abandoned the game.

On the way out of the building Elvis sat down at a piano and sang. After a couple of familiar gospel standards, he launched into "Blue Eyes Crying in the Rain," a song that had recently been a hit for Willie Nelson. It would be the last song Elvis sang.

Each night it took a large quantity of pills to get Elvis anywhere close to sleeping and, returning to his bedroom, he swallowed the first of three packets of pills containing Seconal, Placidyl, Valmid, Tuinal, Demerol, and other depressants and placebos prescribed for him every night by Dr. Nick. A few hours later, still unable to sleep, he took the second packet.

Elvis called down for the third packet a few hours later but everyone had gone, including the nurse who stayed at the house on Dr. Nick's behalf to dispense the singer's drugs. So Elvis asked his aunt Delta to call the nurse, who then got her husband to bring the packet to Graceland.

Elvis told his aunt that he would be getting up at around seven o'clock that evening and a short while later, still unable to sleep, he told Ginger that he was going to the bathroom to read.

At around 1:30 P.M. Ginger woke up and called her mother, who asked how Elvis was. But she did not know, she told her, as he had not come back to bed. She washed, put makeup on and then knocked on his bathroom door. There was no answer. She pushed the door open. Elvis lay on the floor, gold pyjama bottoms around his ankles, his face buried in a pool of vomit. She immediately called downstairs for help.

Al Strada and Elvis's cousin Joe came running upstairs and Joe tried to revive him, but to no avail. The room quickly filled with people, including Elvis's father, Vernon.

The King of Rock and Roll's face was swollen and purple, his tongue was discolored and sticking out of his mouth, his eyeballs were red.

Sometime on the morning of August 16, 1977, Elvis Presley had left the building.

THE FUNERAL

Elvis was taken from the hospital to the Memphis Funeral Home where he was embalmed. He was buried on August 17 dressed in a white suit, white tie, and a blue shirt. He had on a gold TCB ("taking care of business") lightning bolt ring and was in a nine hundred-pound steel-lined copper coffin, flown in from Oklahoma.

The funeral service took place at the Wooddale Church of Christ with music provided by the old-fashioned quartet singers that Elvis grew up with. J.D. Sumner and the Stamps, the Statesmen, Jake Hess, and James Blackwood all performed. Televangelist Rex Hubbard said a few words and Reverend C.W. Bradley presided.

A hundred vans carried the floral tributes to Forest Hill Cemetery, taking nearly four hours. The copper coffin was borne in a white hearse, flanked by a police motorcycle escort. A silver Cadillac then led 17 white limousines along roads lined with crowds of weeping people. Elvis's coffin was placed in a gray, marble-faced mausoleum a short distance from the grave of his mother.

POST MORTEM

Elvis's room was immediately cleaned up, the bed stripped and remade, the bathroom scrubbed. Not even the most common household remedies were to be found in the medicine cabinet. However, Shelby County Medical Investigator Dan Warlick reported seeing two empty syringes in the room.

According to the autopsy, the results of which were announced very soon—too soon, some would say—after Elvis's demise, "death was due to cardiac arrhythmia due to undetermined heartbeat." Two months later, the lab reports and analyses that were filed gave "polypharmacy" as the more likely cause of death. The Laboratory BioSciences report—giving the deceased's name as "Ethel Moore"—listed 14 drugs present in his system. There was ten times the safe level of codeine, Quaalude in a toxic amount, and other drugs at unsafe levels. The arguments about what actually killed Elvis rage on to this day.

As news of Elvis's death began to spread, the local telephone system collapsed under the weight of calls; the local florist received three thousand orders; and a crowd of fifty thousand people gathered on Elvis Presley Boulevard outside Graceland.

As some thirty thousand people—including Caroline Kennedy and James Brown—shuffled into the vestibule of Graceland for the public viewing of the body, police helicopters hovered over the mansion and the National Guard was called out to help the eighty policemen and forty sheriff's deputies trying to control the hysterical crowd.

Elvis Presley's star is undiminished in death and in 2004, daughter Lisa Marie cut a deal with Robert F.X. Sillerman and his new media and entertainment company, CKX, Inc., to sell a majority interest in the assets comprising the estate of Elvis Presley. Sillerman paid about $100 million for 85 percent of Lisa Marie Presley's interests in Elvis Presley Enterprises.

THE CONSPIRACY THEORY

Rumors abound that Elvis is still alive, having faked his death so that he could enjoy a normal life, and there have been numerous sightings of him over the years. However, when a former employee of the Memphis Funeral Home was asked if he thought Elvis was really dead, he replied, "Absolutely. I shoved the cotton balls up his ass when he was embalmed."

When he was reelected in 1944—he had been president since 1932—it seemed unlikely that Franklin Delano Roosevelt would make it to the end of his unprecedented fourth term in office and by March 1945, he was beginning to pay the price of steering his country through two of its greatest crises—the Depression and the Second World War.

Roosevelt had suffered from poor health for many years. In 1921 he was stricken with poliomyelitis, a viral infection of the nerve fibers of the spinal cord, probably contracted while swimming in stagnant lake water while on holiday. He was from then on effectively paralyzed from the waist down, and used leg braces to walk or give the impression that he was walking.

On the afternoon of March 30, he arrived at what was known as the Little White House in Warm Springs, Georgia for a short break. The Georgia air suited the president and his health usually improved when he was there. This visit was no different and he soon settled into a balanced routine of work and pleasure.

On Monday, April 9, Lucy Rutherford, accompanied by her painter friend Elizabeth Shoumatoff, arrived to spend the final week of the vacation with the president. He had met Lucy when he was assistant secretary of the Navy, and he became quite taken with her. Shoumatoff was to paint a portrait of him during their stay.

On April 11, Roosevelt worked on a draft of his upcoming Jefferson Day speech and around noon the following day, Shoumatoff began work on the portrait. The president sat for her in the living room of the house dressed in a double-breasted gray suit and crimson tie. Surrounded by Lucy and several others, he worked his way through a stack of papers as Shoumatoff sketched.

At around 1 P.M., Roosevelt's butler served lunch. Roosevelt seemed agitated and appeared to flinch visibly in his chair. An assistant asked him if he needed help. Suddenly, the president's head fell forward. Gripping it with his left hand, he whispered, "I have a terrific headache." They were the last words he would utter. He collapsed and lost consciousness.

He was immediately taken to his bedroom and his physician, Dr. Bruenn, who had accompanied him to Warm Springs, was summoned. By this time Roosevelt's breathing had stopped and despite desperate attempts at artificial respiration and an injection of adrenaline into his heart, at 3:35 P.M., Franklin Delano Roosevelt, 32nd president of the United States, was pronounced dead of a massive cerebral hemorrhage at age 63.

THE FUNERAL

Roosevelt's declining health was unknown to the public at large and his death caused an outbreak of shock and grief in the United States and around the world. Roosevelt's body was taken by train eleven hundred miles from Warm Springs to Washington, D.C., and then on to the Roosevelt family estate in New York. His tomb lists only his name and dates of birth and death. Fala, his beloved Scottish terrier, is buried a few yards from him.

POST MORTEM

Vice President Harry Truman arrived at the White House at 5:30 P.M. Within ninety minutes, the Cabinet had been assembled and Truman became the 33rd president of the United States.

News flashes on the radio brought the nation the first news of Roosevelt's death. Listeners to a Tom Mix program on the Mutual Broadcasting System and children listening to the Daniel Boone serial *Wilderness Road* on CBS were shocked by broadcast interruptions announcing the death.

The New York Times editorial statement read: "Men will thank God on their knees a hundred years from now that Franklin Delano Roosevelt was in the White House . . . in that dark hour when a powerful and ruthless barbarism threatened to overrun civilization."

Winston Churchill did not attend Roosevelt's funeral and it is claimed that for that reason, many years later, President Lyndon Johnson did not attend Churchill's funeral.

Within a month of Roosevelt's death, the Allies were claiming victory in Europe.

Elizabeth Shomatoff's portrait was never finished and is unsurprisingly known as *The Unfinished Portrait*.

✠

On January 3, 2000, Roosevelt was named first runner-up (behind Albert Einstein) as *Time* magazine's Man of the Century.

TUPAC SHAKUR

In September 1997, rap artist Tupac Shakur was persuaded to go to Las Vegas by Marion "Suge" Knight, CEO of the infamous rap record label Deathrow Records. Tupac told his girlfriend, Kidada, that he had promised Suge that he would accompany him to a heavyweight fight featuring Mike Tyson at the MGM Grand in Vegas, and that he could not let him down.

At his house in Calabasas they prepared to leave, Kidada packing their suitcases. When she reached for the bulletproof vest that Tupac always wore, he told her not to bring it. "It would be too hot," he said.

Traveling to Vegas by car, they stopped at a gas station where Tupac bought five magazines, all of them about guns. He read these all the way to their hotel, the Luxor, from where they drove to Suge's mansion, where Tupac video-taped the record executive making some phone calls.

The fight that night was between Mike Tyson and Bruce Seldon, Tyson winning by a first-round knockout. Tupac was excited by the fight, "Did you see Tyson do it to him?" he said excitedly. "Tyson did it to him! Did ya'll see that? We bad like that. Come out of prison and now we running shit." He went backstage and congratulated Tyson.

8:45 P.M.: Tupac got into a fight with a man called Orlando Anderson, a member of a rival gang who had recently created trouble for a Deathrow employee. The Deathrow crew joined in and Anderson was beaten to a pulp. The fight, recorded by a CCTV camera, was stopped by hotel security and the victim of the beating, after being held for questioning by the police, was allowed to leave, declining to press charges.

8:55 P.M.: Tupac went back to his hotel. He saw a car belonging to the rap star MC Hammer and went over to tell him about the incident. He boasted that it took Mike Tyson fifty punches to beat Selden but he put his man down with only three punches. At the hotel he told Kidada, "Some nigga started a fight with me for nothin.' Something's up, you stay here," He changed clothes and returned to Suge's house. He was due to perform at a party at Club 662 and had wanted to drive his Hummer, but Suge said that they had things to discuss and persuaded Tupac to ride with him.

10:50 P.M.: They left Suge's mansion in the label-owner's black 1996 BMW 750 sedan with tinted windows. Tupac was in the passenger seat, and a ten-car entourage followed them. Playing very low on the sound system was Tupac's new album, *The Don Killuminati: The 7 Day Theory.*

10:55 P.M.: Tupac rolled down the window and a photographer took their picture at a red light.

11 P.M.: They were stopped on Las Vegas Boulevard by Metro bicycle cops for playing the car stereo too loud and for not having license plates. These were in the trunk of the car. Suge was not cited and he was released a few minutes later.

11:15 P.M.: At a red light on Flamingo Road near the intersection of Koval Lane in front of the Maxim Hotel, two girls distracted Tupac and Suge on the driver's side, and a white four-door late-model Cadillac with California plates pulled up. Tupac had been standing up, the upper part of his body through the sunroof. Two of the four men inside the other car got out and fired 13 rounds from Glock .40-caliber handgun into the passenger side of the car. Tupac desperately tried to get into the back seat, but Suge pulled him down and a bullet bounced off of his right hip bone and hit his lung. He was also hit in his right hand and chest. Suge was hit too, but suffered only a minor head wound.

Immediately after the shooting, the Cadillac headed south on Koval. Suge made a U-turn from the left lane of Flamingo and sped west toward Las Vegas Boulevard, away from the nearest hospital. Suge said that he told Tupac he'd get him to a hospital, and Tupac replied, "I need a hospital? You're the one shot in the head."

Patrol officers on an unrelated call at the Maxim Hotel had heard the gunshots and called for backup. Two other officers followed the BMW, which took a left on Las Vegas Boulevard South. Police reached the car when it was caught in traffic at the intersection of Las Vegas Boulevard and Harmon Avenue. They called an ambulance immediately. Inside, the BMW was covered with blood and pieces of gold from Tupac's jewelery. It also had two flat tires.

As they brought Tupac out of the car and placed him on a stretcher, he was moaning, "I can't breathe, I can't breathe."

The ambulance took the two men to the University of Nevada Medical Center. When the police questioned the bodyguard, they asked if he had shot back, but he said he had left his gun in the other car. The bodyguard thought it was Suge's friends who had shot back at the assailants. Yafeu Fula of Tupac's backup group the Outlaws Immortalz—who was fatally shot at a later date—had been in the car behind the BMW with bodyguards. He told the police that he could do a photo lineup, but there were suspicions immediately that the man they had beaten earlier, Orlando Anderson, was behind the shooting.

Tupac lost 22 ounces of blood on the way to the hospital, and as he was being carried to the emergency room he moaned, "I'm dying." He was in critical condition, his injuries including a gunshot wound to his right chest with a massive hemothorax and a gunshot wound to the right thigh. A bullet had also fractured a finger on his right hand.

Just before midnight he was taken to the hospital's trauma center. He was resuscitated in the recovery area and was then placed on life-support machines. Two quarts of blood that had hemorrhaged into his chest cavity were removed. He was taken immediately to the operating room where he underwent emergency surgery. The procedure finished at 2:35 A.M. on September 8.

Another operation began at 6:25 A.M. to remove his punctured right lung in order to stop the internal bleeding. He was back in his room at 7:45 and was put in a medically induced coma and on life-support to take the pressure off his body.

Meanwhile, three sections of the L.A. gang the Bloods met at Lueders Park, and talked about retaliation against the Southside Crips for the attack on Tupac, who was a Blood. At 2:58 P.M. on September 9, a man who Las Vegas police said may have been in the Cadillac was shot in the back on East Alondra.

Tupac opened his eyes once, while Kidada was putting Don McLean's "Vincent" into a cassette player next to his bed. She asked him if he could hear her and told him to move his feet if he did. He moved them. She then asked if he knew she loved him. He nodded. Then he sank into a coma.

On September 11, Bobby Finch, a Southside Crip who Compton police officers said may also have been in the Cadillac, was gunned down on South Mayo at 9:05 A.M. Suge and three lawyers spoke with metro police for an hour but were not much help.

On September 12, Tupac had been due to go to court for sentencing after his conviction for carrying a concealed gun. The next day, doctors tried to resuscitate him several times before his mother, the former Black Panther Afeni Shakur, asked them not to try again.

At 4:03 P.M. on Friday, September 13, Tupac Shakur was pronounced dead of respiratory failure and cardiopulmonary arrest.

THE FUNERAL

Tupac was cremated and his mother spread some of his ashes on a hill in L.A. and some in her garden.

A private funeral was held for him in Las Vegas and on September 15, there was a memorial service for him at the House of the Lord Pentecostal Church in Brooklyn, where he was still listed as a member of the congregation.

Post Mortem

As Tupac lay dying, Suge was ranting at the bodyguard who had forgotten his gun. His threats were interrupted by a phone call informing him that Tupac was dead. Suge then told the bodyguard that it didn't matter now because he was gone, and according to the bodyguard "his voice was cracking up like he was going to cry."

An autopsy determined that Tupac didn't have any illegal drugs in his body, but he had been heavily sedated.

Two detectives took Polaroid pictures of Tupac at the morgue for a police-training book, but these were later removed from the book and destroyed.

Two more Bloods gang members were shot and killed by an assailant who fled on foot.

Police had thought that Anderson could have been a suspect, but he was ruled out because security was still holding him when Tupac had left the building. Anderson was shot dead in Compton in 1999 following a gun battle that left two other men dead.

Because Tupac didn't have a will, Afeni had to file court papers as his only living heir. Deathrow emptied his apartment and took the furniture for which Tupac had been charged over $100,000.

✠

In December 1996, Tupac's new album went platinum.

✠

On the tenth anniversary of Tupac's death, Afeni Shakur met
Nelson Mandela and spread the remainder
of her son's ashes in South Africa.

THE CONSPIRACY THEORY

Rumors persist among fans that Tupac did not actually die.
They are suspicious for a number of reasons:

* No pictures were ever released of Tupac in the hospital.

* Tupac raps about his own funeral on the track "Life
  Goes On."

* The video for the track "Mad at Cha," released a few days
  after his death, shows Tupac as an angel. In the video,
  Tupac was shot after leaving a theater with a friend, which
  is not too dissimilar to how he was shot in real life.

* In the video for "Hail Mary," released under the name
  Makaveli, there is a gravestone that says Makaveli. But the
  gravestone is cracked and there is a hole right in front of
  it, inferring that Makaveli rose from the dead.

* Tupac always wore a bulletproof vest, no matter where he
  went. Why did he not wear it at a very public event like
  the Tyson fight?

* In a number of his songs he talks about being buried, so
  why was he allegedly cremated the day after he "died"?

* Tupac's alias was Makaveli. Machiavelli, the 16th century

Italian philosopher, advocated the staging of one's death in order to evade one's enemies and gain power. Tupac studied Machiavelli in depth while in prison.

* The title of the new album by Makaveli (Tupac) was *The 7 Day Theory*. Tupac was shot on September 7; he survived on the 7th, 8th, 9th, 10th, 11th, 12th, and "died" on September 13. Hence the title, *The 7 Day Theory*.

* Further rumors claim that Tupac was not killed by Orlando Anderson, but that the killing was set up by Suge Knight, who was angry that the rapper was going to leave Deathrow.

DYLAN THOMAS

Where Dylan Thomas is concerned, the glass is, for some, always half-empty—in their opinion he squandered his talent in a sea of alcohol. For others, a man is indivisible from his life and in their minds, Dylan is forever holding a pen in one hand and glass of whiskey in the other. For Dylan, of course, the glass was always full, then empty, then full, and so on.

It was October 1953, and he had not wanted to return to New York so soon. Nonetheless, having already visited in the spring of that year, he found himself there again to take part in a performance of his "play for voices," *Under Milk Wood,* at the Kaufmann Auditorium.

It had been a morose poet who had left London—he gave the thumbs-down sign to his friend Harry Locke as his coach departed Victoria Air Terminal and his mood was not improved by a drunken Irish priest who had to be locked in one of the toilets and was then removed from the plane at a fuel stop in Newfoundland. The fact that by this time Dylan was referring to his wife Caitlin as "my widow" did not bode well for the trip.

He had been ailing for some time, mainly as a result of his excessive drinking and one night as they rehearsed the play, he had taken ill again. His American mistress, Liz Reitell, had brought a friend, Herbert Hannum, along that evening, and as he sat with the poet whose temperature was fluctuating wildly, Hannum covered him with overcoats and provided him with hot water bottles. At one point, Dylan threw up on the green room floor and, as Hannum tried to move him to a couch, the poet grabbed him by the lapels and whispered: "I've seen the gates of hell tonight." The next day, Liz Reitell and Hannum persuaded him to see the doctor who had treated him during his last visit in the spring, Dr. Milton Feltenstein.

It was Dylan's 39th birthday on October 27, an ominous anniversary. He had said ever since he was a boy that he would not live to see forty. Around this time, the poet W.H. Auden spotted him going into the Chelsea Hotel, Dylan's customary residence in New York, and reported that, contrary to reports, he looked neither drunk nor on the verge of death.

But Dylan was still living dangerously, and a detective hired by Time-Life noted that while drinking with a rowdy group of friends, he was seen to take Benzedrine. He was also reported to have pushed a woman out of his cab in the early hours of the morning on his way back to his hotel.

November 3 was Election Day and Dylan expressed his cynicism about politics to a stream of visitors he received in his room. That afternoon he was due to have a meeting with an agent about lecture tours and Liz asked everyone to leave so that she could get Dylan to stop drinking and make him and the room presentable. The meeting was successful, the agent guaranteeing him an income of at least $1,000 while on tour, a decent sum of money back then, and Thomas's biggest break in years.

However, the meeting over, the poet became depressed and lay down on his bed. He started to reminisce to Liz about his hometown, Laugharne, and then announced without warning that he wanted to die. Liz tried to console him, but he began to weep uncontrollably. Eventually he fell asleep, not waking until 2 A.M., then insisting that he had to go out for a drink and to get some air. Liz, exhausted, no longer had the energy to try to stop him.

An hour-and-a-half later, he arrived back, drunk and swaying. "I've had about 18 straight whiskies. I think that's a record." Of course, Dylan was known to exaggerate his drinking, but 18 whiskies or not, it was obvious that, yet again, he had drunk to excess.

He then proceeded to fall asleep, his head in Liz's lap.

When he awoke, he said he could not breathe and insisted on going out. Liz went with him this time to the White Horse Tavern where after only a couple of beers, he told her that he was unwell. Back at the hotel she called Dr. Feltenstein who paid the first of the day's three visits to the hotel. He administered the steroid ACTH, but the poet was still in pain from gastritis and gout.

By the third visit, it was evident from the fact that Dylan was experiencing mild hallucinations that the medication was not working and Liz was convinced he was in the grip of delirium tremens. To calm him, the doctor administered a sedative. Hospital records show he was given half a grain of morphine sulphate—an unusually high dose and potentially lethal, given the poet's breathing complications. It would also have been extremely unusual to administer such a drug to alleviate his gastritis and gout. The doctor has always refused to confirm or deny what he actually gave Dylan that night.

Exhausted, Liz had by now asked the painter Jack Heliker to come and help her care for Dylan. Shortly after he arrived, Dylan began to rave alarmingly about the terrible things tormenting his mind. These were now geometric shapes, he claimed. Jack kept watch as Liz lay down beside Dylan and tried to sleep.

Heliker says that Dylan woke up around midnight, saying, "After 39 years, this is all I've done." Liz, however, maintains that his last words actually were: "Yes, I believe you," in response to her telling him that the horrors rampaging through his mind would disappear.

Suddenly she felt his grip tighten on her hand and Heliker records that his face started to turn blue. Within minutes, the poet was in an ambulance speeding toward the Roman Catholic hospital St. Vincent's. Perhaps, some have said since, Dr. Feltenstein should have sent him there several hours earlier.

He was admitted at 1:58 A.M. and the medical notes state that he arrived in a coma, and that "the impression upon admission was acute alcoholic encephalopathy damage to the brain by alcohol, for which the patient was treated without response."

Poet and critic John Malcolm Brinnin, who had organized Dylan's visit to the States, was called in Cambridge by a hysterical Liz and arrived at St. Vincent's at seven in the morning on November 4. In a coma, Dylan was receiving oxygen and blood transfusions and was diagnosed variously as suffering from liver failure, diabetes, and a vague condition described as "gross insult to the brain." He did not seem to be in danger of death, but his comatose state gave rise to concerns about brain damage when, and if, he came round.

Brinnin called the agent David Higham in London and asked him to tell Caitlin. Ironically, when the message arrived, she was in the midst of a group of friends and neighbors listening to the broadcast of a recording Dylan had made about Laugharne.

Caitlin finally made it to New York on the morning of Sunday, November 8. She was spared immigration at Idlewild Airport thanks to a considerate British Embassy and given a motorcycle escort to St. Vincent's where, on seeing Brinnin, the first thing she is reported to have said was, "Well, is the bloody man still alive?" By this time, a tracheotomy had been performed on the writer, who remained in a coma, and rumors and accusations were flying among the assembled friends and acquaintances.

Caitlin became very agitated on seeing Dylan, emerging from his room after only 15 minutes and banging her head hard on a window. She was taken home by friends of the poet to rest.

Returning that afternoon, she almost pulled Dylan's tubes out as she tried to embrace him and worried the nursing staff by smoking dangerously close to the oxygen tent that surrounded the poet. She was given whiskey to calm her, but instead she became violent, attacking Brinnin and the hospital staff trying to restrain her. She was put in a straitjacket and removed from the hospital to a mental institution for her own safety.

On Monday, November 9, the poet's condition worsened. Fans, most of whom were unknown to Brinnin, filled the hospital waiting room. Once, when Brinnin stepped out into the hospital corridor to get some air, he saw the American poet John Berryman rushing towards him. "He's dead! He's dead!" he shouted. "Where were you?"

Dylan Thomas had died at noon on Monday, November 9, 1953. The postmortem gave the primary cause of death as pneumonia, with pressure on the brain and a fatty liver given as contributing factors. He left little money and had made no will.

THE FUNERAL

At St. Martin's Church, Caitlin is reported to have been howling like a wolf. When someone offered her a box of chocolates she threw them at the ceiling in a rage. Fights broke out in different parts of town. Someone had tried to break into Dylan's work-shed, looking for souvenirs. One woman was wandering around the town offering herself to any man who would have her.

POST MORTEM

The memorial service was held at St Luke's Episcopal Church, New York, on Friday, November 13.
Over four hundred people attended.
That afternoon the body was put on the liner, SS *United States*. Friends, armed with champagne, remained with Caitlin in her cabin until the ship left. By this time, she said, she was "mad, drunk, and heartbroken." She ordered five double whis-kies in the ship's bar and sat down and drank them slowly. She then leaped up and executed what she later described as a "mad dance of destruction," sweeping glasses off tables and doing high kicks, splits, and cartwheels among the debris. The captain

got some seamen to take her down to a bunk in the hold where she found some of the sailors playing cards on Dylan's coffin.

"Dylan would have liked that," she thought.

At Southampton docks, her friend Billy Williams was waiting with a vehicle to transport Caitlin and the coffin back to Laugharne. On the way, they stopped at several pubs and then some hours later, found themselves in Devon,

having taken a wrong turn.

In his final years, Hunter S. Thompson had retreated to what he always termed a "fortified compound" near Aspen, Colorado. His Woody Creek hideout became a destination for actors such as Johnny Depp, Benicio del Toro, and Sean Penn, but Thompson was generally thought to have lost his literary momentum in recent times. Two plastic hips and illness had not helped, even though his weekly column for the ESPN website enjoyed some moments that recalled the highpoints of his "gonzo" style of the sixties and seventies.

He was reported to be in despair over the November 2004 reelection of George W. Bush. "There has to be some defense against having this government in vain seize, take over, invade our lives and our personal privacy every day," he said in an interview early in 2005.

In spite of all this, Hunter had been in fairly good spirits. As ever, he was living at a different time than everyone else, waking up in the late afternoon and beginning the regime of drugs and drink that had fortified him for many years. Now and then he would grab one of his beloved guns and go out and shoot something. Several years before his demise, he had mistakenly shot and wounded his assistant.

He would write and make calls and send faxes to his friends. Occasionally, in the middle of the night, he would call his old partner in crime, the illustrator Ralph Steadman, at his home in

Kent—his "castle," as Hunter called it—and talk about working together one last time.

It was a Sunday, and his son Juan was visiting. Hunter had gone into the next room to telephone his wife, Anita. She says her husband had asked her to come home from the health club she was visiting so they could work on his weekly column. "I was on the phone with him," she reported. "He set the receiver down and he did it. I heard the clicking of the gun." She then said she heard a loud, muffled noise, but did not know what had happened. "I was waiting for him to get back on the phone," she said.

Juan Thompson, in the next room, heard the bang but believed that it was just a book falling.

According to the sheriff's report, Thompson's body was found in a chair by the kitchen table. On the table was a typewriter in which a single sheet of paper had been lined up. The last written word of the writer of *Fear and Loathing in Las Vegas* will in all likelihood puzzle literary experts for years to come. In the center of the page was typed the word "counselor."

THE FUNERAL

The Thompson family canceled plans for a public funeral in favor of a private ceremony. A wake, attended by Jann Wenner, Jack Nicholson, Benicio del Toro, Johnny Depp, Sean Penn, and Ralph Steadman was held in Aspen two weeks after Thompson's suicide.

On August 20, 2005, Thompson's ashes were fired from a cannon atop a 153-foot high tower across a Colorado valley.

The cannon, designed by Thompson and Ralph Steadman in the 1970s, was in the shape of a double-thumbed fist clutching a peyote button. "Mr. Tambourine Man" by Bob Dylan, his favorite song, was played during the proceedings. Among the two hundred-eighty people who attended the ceremony were unsuccessful presidential candidate Senator John Kerry; former senator and unsuccessful presidential candidate George McGovern; actors Sean Penn, Josh Hartnett, and Bill Murray; singers Lyle Lovett and John Oates; and *60 Minutes* correspondent Ed Bradley, who would himself die the following year.

Post Mortem

A number of shots heard around the time that Thompson's body was discovered can be explained by the fact that after discovering the body, Juan Thompson walked outside the house and fired three shotgun blasts into the air, later saying he had done it "to mark the passing of my father."

✠

A letter, described by family and police as a suicide note, was delivered to Thompson's wife four days prior to his death. It was headed "Football Season is Over" and read: "No More Games. No More Bombs. No More Walking. No More Fun. No More Swimming. 67. That is 17 years past 50. 17 more than I needed or wanted. Boring. I am always bitchy. No Fun—for anybody. 67. You are getting Greedy. Act your old age. Relax—This won't hurt."

✠

Ralph Steadman revealed after the suicide that Thompson had

told him 25 years previously "that he would feel real trapped if
he didn't know that he could commit suicide
at any moment."

THE CONSPIRACY THEORY

It is rumored that at the time of his suicide, Thompson was working on two incendiary stories. The first claimed that 9/11 was caused not by planes crashing into the World Trade Center but by explosives in the foundations. Alternatively, it was reported that he had discovered evidence of a pedophile ring in Washington, and had evidence implicating senior U.S. politicians. Was Thompson murdered because he knew too much about one or both of these stories and was about to expose them?

There was something odd about the gun Thompson used to kill himself. In his report, Deputy Ron Ryan noted that the semi-automatic Smith & Wesson model 645 found next to Thompson's body was in an unusual condition. There was a spent shell casing, but although there were six bullets left in the gun's clip, there was no bullet in the firing chamber, as there should have been under normal circumstances. However, a spent bullet was found in the stove hood behind the body.

Thompson is reported to have telephoned a friend the night before his death, sounding scared. He told him about the World Trade Center story and claimed that someone was out to stop him from publishing it. "They're gonna make it look like suicide," he is reported to have said.

ANDY WARHOL

A ndy Warhol worried about death. "Dying is the most embarrassing thing that can ever happen to you," he wrote in his last book, *America*, "because someone's got to take care of all your details, someone's got to take care of the body, make the funeral arrangements, pick out the casket and the service and the cemetery and the clothes for you to wear and get someone to style you and put on the makeup. You'd like to help them, and most of all you'd like to do the whole thing yourself, but you're dead so you can't."

On January 22, 1987, just under a month before it would become redundant, the extraordinary silver-gray wig of Andy Warhol made an appearance at the Credito Valtellinese Gallery in Milan, where an exhibition of his *Last Supper* series was opening to great acclaim. Televison lights lit up the crowds of people who filled the Palazzo della Stellina in expectation of seeing the artist. Despite the glamour and glitz, however, all was not well and Andy retired to his suite in the Hotel Principe e Savoia well before midnight. He was in great pain and languished in his room for the remaining two days of his stay in Italy.

The pain came from enlarged gallstones from which he had been suffering for some time. Toward the end of 1986 he had been warned that they had become so enlarged that failure to have them removed could endanger his life. Andy, however, had a paranoid fear of hospitals and refused to acknowledge the problem for fear it would mean hospitalization. Now, the pain was becoming more than he could bear. He was even curtailing his social life and for Andy Warhol, that was unheard of.

He had recently been receiving treatment to remove his facial lines from a dermatologist, Dr. Karen Burke, and on February 14, he turned to her for help, pleading for the addictive pain relief drug Demerol to ease his condition. Burke refused to supply him with the drug and instead told him she would give him the much weaker Tylenol with codeine, but even then, only on the condition that he see another physician, Dr. Clement Barone, for a sonogram on his right side. Still, the artist demurred.

He spent the weekend of February 14 and 15 in bed but felt no improvement. He decided to try a Shiatsu massage from Linda Li of Li Chiropractic Healing Arts Clinic. But this failed to provide him with the relief he sought and, if anything, made the pain even worse.

On the Tuesday, he was booked to do a catwalk show with the great jazz trumpeter Miles Davis at The Tunnel, a recently opened New York club. Kept waiting in extreme pain in a cold dressing room for an hour before he went on, Andy still managed to put on a good show, clowning around with Davis. But as soon as the left the stage, he collapsed into the arms of his friend Stuart Pivar, gasping, "I feel like I'm gonna die!"

The next afternoon, Andy finally gave in and went to see his doctor, Dr. Denton Cox, where another sonogram confirmed Karen Burke's diagnosis. Cox informed him that his gallbladder was seriously infected and in danger of becoming gangrenous.

He told him he would have to have it removed. On Thursday, another sonogram persuaded Andy that he finally had to do something, especially as he had caught a chill that was making his condition even worse.

On Friday, February 20, Andy's diary showed an appointment to act as a model at the New York Academy of Art. This was hastily canceled and he checked into the New York Hospital under the alias "Bob Robert," having had the alias he had first jokingly suggested—"Barbara"—turned down. On his admittance form he listed his name of him as his maximum Fred Hughes It is an indication of his obsessive nature that when asked for his Blue Cross number—his health insurance number —Andy knew it by heart. The operation was to take place on Saturday and he would be out of the hospital the next day. No one was to know, not even his closest family.

The operation lasted from 8:45 A.M. until 12:10 P.M. There were no complications and after spending three hours in the recovery room, he was wheeled into a private room on the 12th floor of the part of the hospital known as Baker Pavilion. There, he was to be cared for by a private-duty nurse named Min Chou and not by a team of staff nurses. The doctors examining him found everything to be proceeding normally and Andy was reported to be in good spirits, passing the time watching television and gossiping on the phone with his housekeeper, Paige Powell.

At 11 that night, Min Chou reported to the chief surgical resident that Andy's blood pressure was stable. However, at 5:45 the next morning, his pulse suddenly weakened and he began to turn blue. Min Chou desperately tried to wake him but, unable to do so, called for help. For the next 45 minutes doctors tried to revive him, even inserting a tube down his throat to ease his breathing, but by then, rigor mortis had set in.

At 6:21 A.M. on February 22, 1987, Andy Warhol was pronounced dead. He had been famous for slightly more than 15 minutes, and in the hospital he had kept his wig on at all times, even during the operation.

THE FUNERAL

A viewing was held at the Thomas P. Kunsak Funeral Home in Pittsburgh. Andy wore a black cashmere suit, a paisley tie, a platinum wig, and sunglasses. In his hands he held a small prayer book and a red rose. His casket was made of bronze, with gold-plated rails and white upholstery.

The funeral service took place at the Holy Ghost Byzantine Catholic Church, his coffin covered with white roses and asparagus ferns. He was buried in St. John Divine Cemetery in Bethel Park, Pittsburgh. Before the casket was lowered, Paige Powell dropped the latest issue of his magazine, *Interview*; an *Interview* T-shirt; and a bottle of Estée Lauder perfume into the grave.

There was a memorial service on April 1 at Manhattan's St. Patrick's Cathedral at which Yoko Ono delivered a eulogy. After the service, the guests, including Roy Lichtenstein, Keith Haring, Liza Minnelli, and Don Johnson enjoyed lunch at the Diamond Horseshoe while Velvet Underground recordings played in the background. Factory technician and photographer Billy Name drew band members Lou Reed and John Cale into conversation with each other, easing the tension that had existed between them since their musical break up. The result was their collaboration, *Songs for Drella*, a tribute to Andy Warhol, which was released in April 1990 and which eventually led to the Velvet Underground getting back together.

POST MORTEM

Following Andy's death, the district attorney investigated his death but decided that there was no evidence of criminal irresponsibility. However, an investigation by the New York State Department of Health concluded that "the active medical staff of the hospital did not assure the maintenance of the proper quality of all medication and treatment provided to the patient." The Warhol estate brought a wrongful-death lawsuit against the hospital that was settled out of court for three million dollars. The money went to Warhol's two brothers as part of a deal to guarantee that they would not contest Andy's will in which he had left them only $250,000.

The courts conservatively estimated that Andy Warhol's estate was worth over half a billion dollars: $509,979,278, to be precise. This figure was contested by the Warhol Foundation and was subsequently reduced to $228 million—a lower estimate benefited the estate as it meant they would pay lower legal fees and would not have to dole out so much in charitable grants. Bizarrely, to obtain the lesser valuation, the estate argued in court that Warhol was not as great an artist as experts believed him to be. Art dealer André Emmerich testified for the Foundation that Warhol's work was likely to fade into obscurity because the subjects of his paintings—Marilyn Monroe, Elvis Presley, and so on—would eventually be forgotten.

On May 3, 1988, an auction of Andy's effects at Sotheby's was the largest single collection the two hundred fifty-year-old auction house had ever sold, with sixty thousand people viewing it over a ten-day period. People paid fortunes for even insignificant items, including his collection of cookie jars. The auction raised a phenomenal $25,313,238.

DENNIS WILSON

He was the pretty one of the Beach Boys, but Dennis Wilson was also famously—and ironically—the only member of the group that rode on an early sixties wave of surf music who actually enjoyed surfing.

Following the glory years of teen adulation, however, his life had held nothing but disappointment. He had become entangled with Charles Manson and his murderous followers and then his film debut, starring alongside Warren Oates and James Taylor in the road movie *Two Lane Blacktop* (1971), had failed to set the world on fire. Unfortunately, the same could be said about his solo album, *Pacific Ocean Blue* (1977), which received favorable reviews but failed to sell. Sadly, he became addicted to women, drugs, and booze, each feeding on the other. It became so bad that the other Beach Boys told him if he did not clean up they would ban him from touring with them. He needed the money the tours would bring. His lifestyle had become extravagant and he had been spending around $600,000 a year on fancy cars, diamonds, and furs for the numerous women in his life.

Shortly before Christmas 1983, Dennis was yet again trying to tackle his demons when he checked into rehab at St. John's Hospital Health Center in Santa Monica. He was drinking a bottle of vodka a day by this time and lacing it with a liberal daily intake of cocaine. Doctors there put him on a five-day course of Librium to try to stabilize him so that he could begin the effective 21-day detox program they ran. On Christmas Day he walked out of the hospital, but early the next morning he checked into the Daniel Freeman Marina Hospital in Marina Del Rey. The next day, he checked out again and met up with his fifth wife Shawn Love, allegedly the illegitimate daughter of his cousin and fellow Beach Boy, Mike Love.

It was a pity, because his business manager had promised Dennis he would buy back for him his 62-foot yacht, *Harmony*, if he could stay sober for thirty days. He had once lived on the yacht and loved it almost as much as the women in his life. Short of cash in 1980, however, he had reluctantly been forced to sell it.

Dennis spent the night of December 27 at Marina Del Rey with a friend, Colleen McGovern, on the *Emerald*, a 52-foot sloop owned by his friend Bill Oster. Waking at nine, he started this day the way he had started all the others recently—he drank vodka. Then he and Oster rowed around the harbor, visiting friends and buying cigarettes. They ate turkey sandwiches on Oster's boat and by all accounts, Dennis was happy, having a good time.

He was also pretty drunk—the drinking had carried on through the morning and lunch.

After lunch, he slept for a while before visiting a friend, Lathiel Morris, who lived on a nearby houseboat. They talked about him getting his boat back and about Dennis's forthcoming divorce. Talking about relationships, Dennis told Morris, "I'm lonesome. I'm lonesome all the time."

At three in the afternoon, Dennis was diving into the harbor at the spot where the *Harmony* had once been moored. He had thrown stuff overboard at various times during his relationships and was keen to recover some of it. The first thing he brought up was a picture of an ex-wife that he had tossed overboard during an argument. But the water was cold and he was clad only in cut-off jeans and a face mask. After about twenty minutes he climbed out of the water, shivering violently. After warming up again and wolfing down a sandwich, however, he jumped back in. It was now around four in the afternoon.

About 15 minutes later, Oster saw him blow a few bubbles and swim toward the yacht's dinghy. He was swimming quietly and Oster presumed he was trying to hide from them. But when he failed to emerge from the water again, they became concerned.

Oster flagged down a passing harbor patrol boat and told them of his concerns, but he was still convinced that Dennis was playing a trick on them and had clambered ashore out of sight and even now was seated at a nearby bar drinking vodka. They set out to find him, but he was nowhere to be seen. Meanwhile, divers began to explore the waters around the *Emerald*.

They found him at about 5:30 using a long pole to probe the bottom of the harbor. He was 39 years old, and surf was up.

THE FUNERAL

As with most things involving the brothers Wilson and the Beach Boys, there were bitter arguments about how Dennis would be buried. His wife, Shawn, wanted to have him buried at sea, but his brother Carl made plans for him to be buried at Inglewood Cemetery beside the brothers' father, Murray, who had died ten years previously. Shawn won, as the coroner had to legally release Dennis's body to his next of kin, who was his wife.

Three days after his death, a thirty-minute funeral service was held for him at a cemetery chapel in Inglewood. Present were Dennis's mother, Audree; the remaining Beach Boys and close associates; Shawn; his first wife, Carol Freedman, and her 21-year-old son, Scott, from a prior marriage; Dennis's oldest child, 16-year-old Jennifer; his second wife, Barbara Charren, and their sons, Carl and Michael, ages 12 and 11; and Karen Lamm, who Dennis married twice in the late seventies. After the funeral service a wake was held at the house of one of the Beach Boys's management team.

Mike Love, a strict non-drinking vegetarian, turned up with four bottles of the most expensive champagne he could find because, he said, "Dennis would have wanted it that way." He played basketball with Brian Wilson that afternoon and they discussed writing a song for Dennis.

On January 4, three boats containing the Wilson family and friends went to sea with Dennis Wilson's body and he was put to rest in the place he loved best.

POST MORTEM

When they told Charles Manson in prison that Wilson had drowned, he commented, "Wilson was killed by my shadow because he took my music and changed the words from my soul."

NATALIE WOOD

I n the autumn of 1981, Natalie Wood was starring in a
science fiction film called *Brainstorm* with Christopher
Walken. She and her husband, Robert Wagner—she was in her
second marriage to the *Hart to Hart* actor—invited Walken to
spend Thanksgiving weekend with them on board their 55-foot
cabin cruiser, the *Splendor*. They planned to spend the holiday
weekend cruising off the Los Angeles coast of California.

On the first day of the cruise, November 27, their one-man
crew of Captain Dennis Davern piloted the boat to Catalina
Island where they put down anchor. Waking from their naps
before Wagner, Wood and Walken sailed the yacht's dinghy
ashore and drank for a couple of hours in a Catalina restaurant
where Wagner later joined them for dinner and more drinks.
They returned to the *Splendor* at 10 P.M., already quite drunk,
and resumed their drinking onboard.

Wagner's complaints that his wife spent too much time on
her acting career and not enough time looking after their children turned into an argument. Walken sided with Wood and as
the drinks flowed, the argument raged into the night.

The next day, the *Splendor* put down anchor at Isthmus Cove.
The trio dined that evening at the Harbor Reef Restaurant,
beginning at four in the afternoon with several bottles of champagne and causing a disturbance in the restaurant, where, it is

claimed, Natalie had been openly flirting with Walken. Leaving the restaurant very drunk, they clambered aboard their small dinghy and returned to the *Splendor*. Things become unclear at this point, but what is certain is that as Captain Davern began to shut the boat down for the night, the three continued to party.

At around 12:20 A.M., Davern noticed that the boat's dinghy was missing. He knew that Natalie often took it to view the evening sky away from the boat and presumed that this was what had happened. But, when she failed to return, Davern became worried and informed Wagner who immediately jumped into a second dinghy and went to look for her.

The coroner later suggested a likely version of the night's tragic events. Wood had indeed gone out in the dinghy but had then slipped and fallen into the water. Desperately, she had tried to crawl up the sides of the rubber dinghy, but the heavy coat she was wearing as protection against the night chill became sodden with water, and soon weighed thirty to forty pounds, prevented her from getting into the boat. As she had struggled to get into the dinghy, it had started to drift slowly out into the harbor. Becoming frightened, she had begun to scream but her yells had been drowned out by the noise of a loud stereo on a boat nearby. She had grabbed the side of the dinghy and had begun to steer it toward the shore but eventually she succumbed to the cold and died, shrouded in her nightgown and red down coat.

She was 43 years old.

The Funeral

Natalie Wood's gardenia-clad casket was buried in Westwood

Village Memorial Park Cemetery in Los Angeles on December 2, 1981. Natasha, Natalie's 11-year-old daughter, requested that diamond earrings be placed on her mother's ears and Robert Wagner insisted on burying her in a fox fur coat that he had not yet given to her.

Numerous celebrities, including Sir Laurence Olivier, Rock Hudson, Gregory Peck, and Elizabeth Taylor attended the funeral, alongside Robert Wagner and Christopher Walken.

Post Mortem

The official coroner's report states that a private searcher who located the dinghy says that the key was in the ignition, which was in the off position. The gear was in neutral and the oars tied down. From this account, it would appear that the boat had not even been used.

Sources close to Robert Wagner insist that Wood drowned when she slipped into the water after becoming annoyed by the incessant pounding of the dinghy tied up on the side of the yacht.

Some reports say that Wagner and Walken had a violent argument that night, that Natalie tried to leave the yacht and accidentally fell overboard. A woman on shore later said she heard cries for help in the water and heard other voices saying they were coming. Wagner, Walken, and the captain of the *Splendor* all deny this.

About The Author

Gordon Kerr has held senior marketing positions with Bloomsbury Publishing (UK) and the book chain Waterstone's. As a marketing consultant, his clients have included The Man Booker Prize and the British Museum, among others. He has worked with Ralph Steadman on three of his titles, including *The Joke's Over*, his book on Hunter S. Thompson.